DEDICATIONS

To my husband, Adam,
thank you for your
kindness and patience,
as well as tech support,
nonstop cheering on, and
happinesses. Let's put up
more nest boxes together.

—*Margaret A. Barker*

Thanks to my husband,
Steve, and daughter,
Liliana Pearl, for adding
sweetness to my life that
soars higher than the birds.
Your wondrous presence
makes my Ithaca-based
nest box cavity complete.

—*Elissa Wolfson*

Quarto is the authority on a wide range of topics.

Quarto educates, entertains and enriches the lives of
our readers—enthusiasts and lovers of hands-on living.

www.quartoknows.com

First published in 2013 by Voyageur Press, an imprint of Quarto Publishing Group
USA Inc., 400 First Avenue North, Suite 400, Minneapolis, MN 55401 USA.
Telephone: (612) 344-8100 Fax: (612) 344-8692

quartoknows.com

Visit our blogs at quartoknows.com

Voyageur Press titles are also available at discounts in bulk quantity for industrial or
sales-promotional use. For details write to Special Sales Manager at Quarto Publishing
Group USA Inc., 400 First Avenue North, Suite 400, Minneapolis, MN 55401 USA.

ISBN: 978-0-7603-4220-6

Library of Congress Cataloging-in-Publication Data
Barker, Margaret A.
  Audubon birdhouse book : building, placing, and maintaining great homes for great
birds / by Margaret A. Barker and Elissa Wolfson.
    pages cm
  Includes bibliographical references and index.
  ISBN 978-0-7603-4220-6 (softcover)
  1. Birdhouses--Design and construction. 2. Bird attracting--United States. I.
Wolfson, Elissa. II. Title.
  QL676.5.B257 2013
  728'.927--dc23
                                    2013018947

Editor: Elizabeth Noll
Design Manager: James Kegley
Layout: Diana Boger
Design: Karl Laun

Front matter photos (in order from frontispiece): male Prothonotary Warbler, Mark Musselman;
male Eastern Bluebird, David Kinneer; one-day-old Wood Duck chick, Roger Strand,
courtesy of the Wood Duck Society; American Kestrel nest box, Richard M. Tuttle;
Ash-throated Flycatcher, Steve Simmons; Loon chick and parent, Derrick Z. Jackson;
male Pileated Woodpecker male and chick, Ruhikanta Meetei; Eastern Bluebird male
and fledgling, David Kinneer
Front cover photo: David Kinneer
Back cover photos (top to bottom): male Mountain Bluebird, Myrna Pearman, courtesy of
Ellis Bird Farm, Alberta, Canada; male Hooded Merganser, Ashok Khosla; female American
Kestrel, Paul Spurling, courtesy of the Peregrine Fund/Americana Kestrel Partnership

Range maps provided by the Cornell Lab of Ornithology.

Printed in China

Audubon®

BIRDHOUSE BOOK

Building, Placing, and Maintaining Great Homes for Great Birds

By Margaret A. Barker and Elissa Wolfson

Foreword by Stephen W. Kress, vice president for bird conservation for the National Audubon Society

Carpentry by Chris Willett

Voyageur Press

CONTENTS

FOREWORD:

WOODPECKERS: THE ORIGINAL

BIRDHOUSE BUILDERS 6

ACKNOWLEDGMENTS 8

CHAPTER 1:

MANY BIRDS NEED A HELPING HAND 10

CHAPTER 2:

BUILD HOMES TO BENEFIT BIRDS 18

CHAPTER 3:

BIRDS IN BOXES 32

    Wrens (Bewick's, Carolina, House) 34

    Warblers (Prothonotary) 40

    Bluebirds (Eastern, Western, Mountain) 46

    Flycatchers (Ash-throated, Great Crested) 57

    Swallows (Tree, Violet-green) 59

    Titmice (Tufted, Oak, Juniper,

        Black-crested) 61

    Owls (Barred) 64

    Owls (Eastern Screech, Western Screech) 71

    Flickers (Northern) 78

    Owls (Barn) 84

    Kestrels (American) 91

    Chickadees (Black-capped, Carolina,

        Mountain) 99

    Ducks (Wood Duck) 106

    Mergansers (Hooded) 112

    Swallows (Purple Martin) 114

CHAPTER 4:

BIRDS OUTSIDE OF BOXES 120

Doves (Mourning) 122

Swallows (Barn) 126

Robins (American) 129

Finches (House) 134

Phoebes (Eastern, Say's) 136

Owls (Burrowing) 138

Loons (Common) 141

Swifts (Chimney) 143

Herons (Great Blue) 146

Ospreys 149

CHAPTER 5:

HOW TO HELP THE BIRDS 152

BIBLIOGRAPHY 156

INDEX 157

ABOUT THE TEAM 160

LIST OF BUILDING PLANS

Carolina Wren nest box 37

Prothonotary Warbler nest box 42

Xbox (for bluebirds, flycatchers,
    swallows, and titmice) 52

Barred Owl nest box 66

Screech-Owl nest box 74

Bower Flicker box 80

Barn Owl nest box 86

American Kestrel nest box 94

Chickadee nest box 102

Wood Duck nest box (for Wood Ducks
    and Hooded Mergansers) 108

Purple Martin gourd rack 117

Mourning Dove nest basket 124

Barn Swallow L-shaped platform 128

V-shaped shelf (for American Robins,
    House Finches, and Phoebes) 130

Covered shelf (for American Robins,
    House Finches, and Phoebes) 132

WOODPECKERS:
THE ORIGINAL BIRDHOUSE BUILDERS

Building a nest box for wild birds can be one of the most gratifying projects a person can undertake. When placed in the proper habitat, a nest box or birdhouse may be occupied, defended, and filled with eggs almost immediately. The best nest boxes are simple, without elaborate detail, void of paint and embellishment. The first nest box builders and skilled construction pros were woodpeckers, making homes by excavating cavities in tree trunks. By observing woodpecker homes, we can learn much about avoiding predators, preventing drainage issues, and locating a nest to minimize the effects of extreme weather. When building a nest box, try to think like a woodpecker.

Woodpeckers help other cavity-nesting birds because of their talent for building ideal homes. A woodpecker pair typically remains together for years, but the male and female chisel separate sleeping places. When nesting season arrives, rather than reuse a previous home, they excavate a new nesting cavity. In this way, each pair typically creates three tree cavities per year for roosting and nesting, all of which they vacate at the end of the breeding cycle. Many other bird species later depend on these various-sized holes, created by different-sized woodpeckers, for their own sleeping and nesting needs. Cavities excavated by Downy Woodpeckers are ideal for chickadees and nuthatches, flicker nest cavities are a good fit for American Kestrels, and Pileated Woodpeckers can hammer out housing large enough for Bufflehead Ducks. Unfortunately, the young forests that prevail over much of North America are not ideal for woodpeckers, as they too often lack large, dead, standing trees required for woodpecker drumming. The housing shortage is furthered by nonnative House Sparrows and European Starlings that compete for scarce housing.

Margaret Barker and Elissa Wolfson have provided a much-needed, updated volume on nest boxes by researching and gathering previously scattered recent innovations and some of the most classic designs for birdhouse design and current best practices for placement, mounting, and maintenance. This is important, not just for birdhouse species such as bluebirds and martins, but also for the many species that nest outside of boxes, including Ospreys, loons, American Robins, Mourning Doves, Chimney Swifts, and even Burrowing Owls. In this book, one can find tips for pruning trees and shrubs to make them more appealing for nest builders such as goldfinches, vireos, and most warblers.

With care, woodworkers can provide housing that is nearly as good as natural nesting cavities. In some habitats, everything a bird needs, including food, shelter, and singing posts, may be available—except for a suitable nesting cavity. By installing nest boxes in such otherwise-ideal habitats, people can help to increase the carrying capacity of the land for these birds.

Some birds are now totally dependent on human housing, in part because natural housing is scarce, but also because young birds tend to look for familiar housing. Bluebirds, Purple Martins, and Chimney Swifts now make their nests almost entirely in human-created housing. The responsiveness of these species to human-provided nest boxes has encouraged the formation of organizations, websites, publications, and most important, passionate and creative birdhouse builders who are constantly tinkering, with the goal of building increasingly better nest boxes.

The boxes and nesting structures described here are the results of decades of caring field-testing, sometimes by groups of amateur carpenters and bird aficionados, culminating in designs such as the "Xbox," a recent state-of-the-art bluebird box. This innovative design challenges some of the classic rules of birdhouse building, such as required drainage holes. New methods provide adjustable ventilation depending on season, location, and latitude. Other new ideas shared here are based on astute observations of bird behavior, such as Dick Tuttle's clever kestrel box with pseudo-holes on two side walls to help attract cavity-seeking birds from varied angles, an idea that may eventually prove useful for other species as well. These latest plans offer significant improvements over older designs; many are easier to build, install, and clean. Most important, they offer housing that is more adaptable to extreme weather and safer from predators.

Just as there are advances in basic birdhouse design, technology is also providing new ways to attract, study, and conserve birds. Social attraction, a method developed for attracting seabirds to nesting islands, is now being used to attract songbirds to backyards. In this way, playback recordings of Purple Martin "dawn songs," coupled with martin decoys, can help to advertise new housing. Likewise, Barn and Cliff Swallows are also responsive to audio calls, encouraging nesting in otherwise unoccupied barns and eaves. Like seabirds, these birds nest in colonies, but there is increasing evidence that most young songbirds looking for new homes will recognize songs of their own species and choose to nest nearby, providing they find suitable habitat.

Technology is also allowing remarkable views of birds within their nests. This book includes information on nest cameras that offer intimate views of birds ranging from hummingbirds to eagles. High-definition bird cams reveal details about the family lives of birds previously hidden in nest boxes, from the treetop nests of owls to the underground burrows of puffins on remote islands. These nest cams are enabling citizen scientists everywhere to watch and record the details of nesting behavior and report them to groups like Audubon and the Cornell Lab of Ornithology. By gathering information about the timing of bird breeding and even the kinds of foods delivered to chicks, these observations help us understand climate change, and ultimately, the state of our planet's health.

Certainly the process of improving nest boxes and nesting structures, and watching the birds within them, will continue. For example, while testing the construction

methods presented in this book, master birdhouse builder Chris Willett designed a wooden chickadee box shaped like a tree stump. This elegant nest box will likely prove popular with chickadees, titmice, nuthatches, and wrens, and it's all because woodpeckers inspired Willett's thinking.

—Stephen W. Kress
Vice president for bird conservation
for the National Audubon Society
Ithaca, New York

ACKNOWLEDGMENTS

Over the course of researching and writing the *Audubon Birdhouse Book*, it has been our good fortune to encounter many generous and passionate people working on behalf of birds. Bird "landlords," those who offer housing and keep watch on "their" birds, conservationists, woodworkers, researchers, nest box designers, and photographers—all have shared their skills and knowledge to inform this book.

Speaking first with North American Bluebird Society (NABS) board member Dan Sparks of Indiana was an invaluable stepping-off point that led to contacts with other veteran "bluebirders," including NABS president Sherry Linn and current NABS board members Bet Zimmerman and Tom Comfort, who were patient and candid in answering our many questions.

Other NABS members and bluebirders who passed along bird wisdom include Vicki Butler, Steve Gilbertson, and Steve Eno of Bluebirds Across Nebraska. Keith Kridler, co-author of the *Bluebird Monitor's Guide*, was always there with a Texas perspective. Myna Pearman weighed in with Mountain Bluebird advice and beautiful photographs. Keith Radel of the Bluebird Recovery Program of Minnesota provided valuable input and historical views. Georgia woodworker and Xbox plan draftsman Fred Stille shared woodworking tips and nest box building stories.

Besides the X-Men, who designed the bluebird Xbox—Kevin Berner, Tom Comfort, Steve Eno, Steve Gilbertson, Keith Kridler, Keith Radel, and Dan Sparks—we highlight other nest box designers. Retired science teacher and bluebirder Dick Tuttle provided the American Kestrel nest box design and educated us about his kestrel work in Ohio, even in late-night phone calls. From him, we heard about the late Bob Orthwein's design for Carolina Wrens and Allen Bower's design for Northern Flickers. Phone conversations with Allen were always instructive and his detailed notes and "snail mail" letters most appreciated.

The Purple Martin Conservation Association (PMCA) steered us to our two Purple Martin housing designers, just the kinds of designs we had been hoping for. Ron Seekamp's Purple Martin house woodworking plans focus on larger nesting compartments but fewer of them per house. Chuck Abare's simple wooden gourd rack design accommodates both natural and modern plastic gourds. The PMCA staff was generous with their time, especially executive director John Tautin, Louise Chambers, and Tara Dodge.

We found nest boxes for three owl species. California woodworker and bird-bander extraordinaire Steve Simmons, who designed the Barn Owl nest box, has also been busy helping Ash-throated Flycatchers, Western Bluebirds, Burrowing Owls, and Wood Ducks over the past four decades. Rob Bierregaard has introduced North Carolina students and others to the wonders of the suburban Barred Owl. He refined his nest box design to study how Barred Owls survive and "make a living" in suburbia. Fred Gehlbach, who wrote the Eastern Screech-Owl species account for *Birds of North America Online*, has studied both Eastern and Western Screech-Owls. His nest box design is the result of investigating natural tree cavities.

Long-term Prothonotary Warbler studies begun in the 1980s along the James River near Richmond, Virginia, have shown these warblers use nest boxes—and how! Today, more than 600 Prothonotary Warbler nest boxes are set up there, designed by professor Bob Reilly of Virginia Commonwealth University.

Our Wood Duck nest box design was created around 1990 by the late Don "The Duckman" Helmeke, a Minnesota outdoorsman. Wood Duck Society director Roger Strand graciously shared great insights into Wood Duck behavior.

We were privileged to have Canadian Chickadee researchers Ken Otter and Dan Mennill review our chickadee text. Ken edited *The Ecology and Behavior of Chickadees and Titmice* (2007) and Dan coauthored the

Birds of North America Online species account for the Black-capped Chickadee. Both Ken and Dan, professors at universities in British Columbia and Ontario, respectively, are encouraging their students to study and test nest box design.

To find examples of how to help birds that nest "out of the box," we tapped into the Audubon family—local chapters working for birds. Each of our contacts is a story unto itself. For conveying to us your work "in the field," we send special thanks to the following:

- Ascutney Mountain Audubon Society (Vermont): Marianne Walsh and Sam Gordon Gurney
- Audubon Minnesota: Ron Windingstad
- Golden Gate Audubon Society (California): Ilana DeBare
- Lake County Audubon Society (Illinois): Jack Nowak and Chris Geiselhart
- Los Angeles Audubon Society (California): Eleanor Osgood
- Madison Audubon Society (Wisconsin): Pat Ready
- Maine Audubon: Susan Gallo
- Santa Clara Valley Audubon Society (California): Bob Power

Other institutions provided invaluable assistance. The Cornell Lab of Ornithology's Diane Tessaglia-Hymes and Barry Bermudez made sure we got range maps for our species accounts. Charles Eldermire provided Bird Cam images, and NestWatch project leader Jason Martin reviewed copy. Hawk Mountain Sanctuary's Keith Bildstein and Mary Linkevich provided insights and images from their long-term kestrel nest box research. John Sauer and David Ziolkowski Jr. of the U.S. Geological Survey explained North American Breeding Bird Survey results. Lynda Garrett of the Patuxent Wildlife Research Center library located historic documents.

Others who provided key information include Barbara Boyle of the Althea R. Sherman project, George Petrides of the Wild Bird Centers of America, Eric Hanson of the Vermont Center for Ecostudies, Scott Artis of the Burrowing Owl Conservation Network, Steve Parren and John Buck with the Vermont Fish and Wildlife Department, Pat and Bill Stovall of Stovall Products, Clifton Brown and Linda Wiley of the Maryland Wood Duck Initiative, James A. Barker, Jr., Janet Fries, Chris W. Johnson, and Dan Hutchings.

Sincere thanks go out to our talented photographers. Three in particular came to the fore when most needed: Ashok Khosla, David Kinneer, and Mark Musselman. Aaron Ward of the Maryland Wood Duck Initiative sent us a CD with several hundred of his remarkable images.

We are grateful to our editors, Dennis Pernu and Elizabeth Noll, for their vision, commitment, and support to see this project through. Their calm and steady presence kept things moving forward.

Chris Willett, our master woodworker and book project team member, rocks! His bird and woodworking smarts are evident throughout the build sections and final products. We especially appreciated his flexibility when challenged—and the fact that he was fun to work with all along the way.

National Audubon's Stephen Kress provided invaluable guidance throughout the process, which was much welcomed and appreciated.

Our sincere apologies if we have made errors of any sort, or overlooked any individual or organization that helped along the way.

Finally, we learned that though there are differing and sometimes strong opinions about nest boxes and nesting structures, everyone we spoke to had the same goals in mind: to do whatever it takes to ensure the health, safety, and continued future of wild birds. It is our hope that this work will serve to inform and inspire others to build great homes for birds who need them, to carefully place those homes in good habitat, to protect them from predators, to take "landlord" responsibilities seriously, and especially, to learn from and enjoy the birds in your care.

CHAPTER 1

MANY BIRDS NEED A HELPING HAND

I doubt if it ever occurs to the average person that birds are actually in need of nesting sites.

—Ernest Harold Baynes

A flicker feeds its young in a "Berlepsch" nest box, a rustic design that originated from nesting studies conducted by Baron Hans von Berlepsch in Germany. The 1915 photo is from the book *Wild Bird Guests* by Ernest Harold Baynes (1915).

An indomitable bird enthusiast of the early 1900s, Ernest Harold Baynes recognized that most people put up nest boxes simply to have birds around them, to enjoy their song and beauty. Others in his day placed nest boxes in orchards and near field crops in the hopes that bird parents would feed their chicks a steady diet of agricultural pests, thus keeping the insects off the crops. Nearly a century later, many birds do need help finding suitable places to raise their young. Due to both natural and human impacts, those places can be hard to find.

NATURAL IMPACTS ON BIRDS

Severe weather is one of the biggest natural threats birds face. Although some storms create positive changes for birds—such as removing vegetation for birds like terns that require open sand for nesting—the same hurricanes can blow migratory birds way off course and have lasting negative impacts on their habitats. In 1989, Hurricane Hugo decimated the Red-cockaded Woodpecker's old-growth forest habitat in South Carolina when it snapped trees in half. A Canadian Wildlife Service study found that Chimney Swift populations dropped by half the spring following October 2005's Hurricane Wilma, the most powerful hurricane on record in the Atlantic Basin. The full picture of how birds fared during Hurricane Sandy in 2012 may not emerge for some time. In a recent *National Geographic.com Daily News* report, Bryan Watts of the Center for Conservation biology in Williamsburg, Virginia, points out that birds have high mortality rates during events like Hurricane Sandy; those that are migrating are most at risk. He adds that Hurricane Sandy's most lasting effect will likely be "coastal reshaping"—the inundation and subsequent flattening of sand dunes and barrier islands inhabited by coastal bird species. Storms can also connect former islands to the mainland, creating passageways for bird predators like raccoons.

Heavy snow during migration can be devastating. A report in the January 1907 issue of *The Auk*, a publication of the American Ornithologist's Union, described how thousands of birds caught in a snowstorm while migrating across Lake Huron drowned when blown into the water. As many as 5,000 dead birds were counted along the shoreline, including robins, sparrows, and juncos. A more recent northeastern blizzard in March 1993, locally dubbed "the blizzard of the century," affected twenty-six states and eastern Canada, with snow accumulations of up to three feet over several days. Such late winter and early spring storms occur at a time when many birds are beginning to

HUNGRY FOR A PESTICIDE-FREE PLANET

Birds can be victims of pesticide poisoning, or they can provide an alternative to pesticide. One innovative group, the California-based Hungry Owl Project (HOP) distributes a safe rodenticide—live birds. Started in 2001, HOP promotes the use of Barn Owls and other beneficial predators for natural pest control, eliminating the need for toxic chemicals and pesticides. In partnership with the wildlife rehabilitation center WildCare, HOP encourages these predators by building and installing nest boxes and raptor perches. "We believe there are *no* safe rodenticides," says HOP's Alex Godbe. "One poisoned rodent, fed to a nest of Barn Owl chicks, can wipe out the entire nest."

Alternatively, a family of five owls can consume 3,000 rodents in a breeding season. HOP includes school children by making presentations and soliciting their help in building owl boxes. So far, more than 1,000 nest boxes have been installed at ranches, farms, vineyard, and private homes. HOP works with the landowners, putting up and maintaining nest boxes, once the owners agree to stop setting out poisons. "Many vineyards are now growing organically, and owl nest boxes can be an important element of their pest control," says Godbe. "Our goal is to educate and provide alternative methods when possible and help create a "win, win" situation for all." Visit hungryowl.org.

Young members of the Cornfield Bird Club in Cornish, New Hampshire, proudly display their homemade nest boxes in this photo, circa 1915. Boys and girls in classrooms and bird clubs were encouraged to "make nest boxes and food houses" for the "benefit of local birds." (From *Wild Bird Guests*, Ernest Harold Baynes, 1915)

nest and many others are still migrating back to their summer breeding grounds. It is also when food for birds is particularly scarce, as most insects have not yet begun to emerge, and plants have not yet begun to grow. What little food remains for the birds can get buried in ice and snow, which can lead to starvation. Other severe weather, such as droughts and flooding, also makes life hard for birds.

HUMAN IMPACT ON BIRDS

The list of human-created problems for birds is a long one. By far the largest killer of birds in America is the loss of bird habitat to development. This, along with large-scale agricultural land use, has taken a toll on birds, reducing their usable habitat dramatically in some places across North America. Land, water, and air pollution, collisions with windows, cars, cell towers, and power lines, oil spills at sea, and human disturbances at nesting sites, all pose additional major threats to bird populations. The effects of climate change, too, may be substantial.

All of this helps to explain why about a quarter of the 836 species of birds protected under the Migratory Bird Treaty Act are currently in decline. For a third of the remaining birds, there is insufficient information to determine the health of their populations. Although there may not be much individuals can do to effect direct change on global issues, other issues around the home are more easily addressed.

PESTICIDES

According to the Environmental Protection Agency (EPA), agriculture accounts for about 80 percent of all pesticide use each year in the United States (680 million pounds in 2007), and industry and government an additional 12 percent. Individuals in their homes and gardens use about 8 percent—or 66 million pounds— of pesticides annually. Children and pets, due to their smaller body sizes and tendency to play on the ground, have a greater risk of pesticide exposure than adults. Indeed, studies show traces of garden chemicals found in 99 percent of the children tested. In addition, according to the U.S. Fish and Wildlife Service, pesticides directly kill 72 million birds each year. An even larger number may ingest the poisons and die later or leave orphaned chicks to perish.

People can help bring these numbers down by following a few simple steps. Consider using compost rather than commercial fertilizers to help plants grow. Mulch or black plastic sheets can be used instead of herbicides to block weed growth. Nontoxic techniques, such as sticky tapes, pheromone traps, and biological controls can be used against a variety of unwanted insects. Where possible, buy produce from local

Domestic cats are good human companions, but they are still predators. To protect nesting birds, consider keeping cats indoors.
Keith Kridler

and organic farmers who grow food without harmful chemicals. For additional helpful information, and downloadable posters, go to athome.audubon.org.

INTRODUCED SPECIES

Three introduced species in particular can wreak havoc on bird life. They are domestic cats, House Sparrows, and European Starlings.

OUTDOOR CATS

One of the biggest threats to North American birds and other wildlife is outdoor cats. Although recent studies about birds and cats have drawn attention to it, the issue is not new. The "cat question" was discussed often and passionately in the pages of *Bird-Lore*, the predecessor of *Audubon* magazine. In a 1910 issue of *Bird-Lore*, a Missouri gentleman wrote in to complain about cats catching some of his Purple Martins. Similar stories could be found in every issue. Editorials of the day advocated for laws against "vagrant cats," and suggested taxes on house cats.

Government publications, too, mentioned the cat-bird problem in the early twentieth century. In the U.S. Department of Agriculture's *Farmer's Bulletin 609: Bird Houses and How to Build Them* (1914), biologist Ned Dearborn stated, "Cats and large snakes are enemies of birds, the former perhaps killing more birds than any other mammal." A significant study in the late 1980s from ecologist Stan Temple at the University of Wisconsin-Madison showed each outdoor cat killed an average of five to six birds a year. Yet through the years and with even more studies, the problem of wild birds and domestic cats remains unresolved.

In 2013, scientists from the Smithsonian's Conservation Biology Institute and the U.S. Fish and Wildlife Institute found that outdoor cats kill a median of 2.4 billion birds in the United States annually—a mortality rate higher than previously thought. Nesting birds, including migratory birds that may travel thousands of miles to breed near our homes, are especially vulnerable. So are stunned, but still living birds that have collided with windows and fallen to the ground, within reach of outdoor cats.

To keep birds in nest boxes as safe as possible from outdoor cats, it may be necessary to use predator guards (explored further in Chapter 2). Other recommendations include educating neighbors about the impacts of roaming cats, making sure backyard feeder and nest box birds have nearby brush piles and trees into which birds can escape, keeping areas directly under nest boxes mowed and free of hiding places, and spaying or neutering all cats, particularly those allowed outside. Cat fences and enclosures, too, can dissuade and prevent cats from visiting nest boxes (see details on cat enclosures in Chapter 2).

HOUSE SPARROWS AND EUROPEAN STARLINGS

Much has been said, written, and uttered in expletives about two nonnative birds that have changed the avian world in North America: the House Sparrow and the European Starling.

The House Sparrow (*Passer domesticus*) arrived here first. Formerly called the English Sparrow, it is actually not a sparrow but a weaver finch, native to Asia, North Africa, Europe, and the British Isles. More than 200 years ago, there were no House Sparrows in North America. Today, their population in North America is estimated to be more than 150 million.

The bird was first brought to the United States in 1850 and released by well-meaning people who had heard that the "English Sparrow" might control insects. The population took hold in 1851, when Nicholas Pike, then-director of the Brooklyn Institute, brought House Sparrows back from a trip to Liverpool, England. Half were released somewhere in New York City upon arrival; the other half was set free in the city's Greenwood Cemetery in 1852. Other releases followed across the county, and by the end of the century, the House Sparrow's population was already considered a threat to native birds.

The first volume of *Bird-Lore* magazine, published in 1899, carried many references to the problem of House Sparrows. In that issue, the Connecticut Audubon Society reported that its next year's work would include "the consideration of a practical method for destroying the English Sparrow, as a bird distinctly injurious to song birds and others having agricultural value." In the magazine's next

issue, a Connecticut reader described his new rough board "sparrow-proof" bluebird house. Massachusetts ornithologist Edward Howe Forbush, in his state-produced publication *Bird Houses and Nesting Boxes* (1915), predicted, "The European House Sparrow is the greatest and most ubiquitous enemy of all native birds that nest in bird houses and nesting boxes."

After peaking in the 1920s, House Sparrow populations began to decline, especially in cities. The birds had been feeding abundantly on spilled grain meant for carriage horses, but now automobiles were beginning to replace horses for transportation. Today, House Sparrow populations are steady and widespread across North America. They out-compete many native species for places to nest, including birds in nest boxes and other artificial nesting structures. House Sparrows are aggressive and highly protective of their chosen nest site. They can kill adult birds and nestlings and destroy eggs.

In 2005, the U.S. and Canadian starling population was estimated to be 140 million birds—nearly half of the global total of 310 million. These introduced birds, named for their starry plumage, can be dissuaded from using nest boxes meant for native birds by creating access holes smaller than the one-and-a-half-inch diameter they need to enter. *Ashok Khosla*

A male House Sparrow. These small birds can cause big problems for native cavity nesters. The first House Sparrows introduced to North America from England were released in New York City in the early 1850s; they are now one of the most abundant birds in North America. *Ashok Khosla*

Fig. 159.

Fig. 162.

Fig. 160.

Fig. 163.

Fig. 161.

Suggestions for home-made bird houses.

Liberty Hyde Bailey, a professor at Cornell University, introduced *Teacher's Leaflets* into rural schools. Pictured here, *The Birds and I: Teacher's Leaflet No. 10*, May 1898. Several of the nest boxes depicted, while well meaning and instructive, are now known to be poor designs. They lack the drainage and ventilation holes important in some regions. All designs also include perches, which make nest boxes easy for predators to access.

Eugene Schieffelin is credited—and blamed—for bringing the European Starling (*Sturnus vulgaris*) to North America. Apparently, Schieffelin, a theater fan, wanted to bring every bird mentioned in Shakespeare's entire works to the United States. He wasn't successful in establishing populations of other birds mentioned by Shakespeare, but the starlings thrived. In 1880 Schieffelin brought in eighty starlings and released them in Central Park. The next year he released forty more. By 1950, starlings were reported in every U. S. state and Canadian province. Today, studies estimate this bird's numbers at 140 million.

Male starlings can be very aggressive when staking out nesting sites, taking over nest boxes even when they are already occupied. Starting in late summer and continuing until breeding time, starlings roost in large groups that can number more than 150,000. As introduced, nonnative species, neither House Sparrows nor starlings are protected by the federal Migratory Bird Treaty Act.

HUMAN HELPERS

The concept of caring for birds in one's own backyard by offering them food at feeders, and shelter in artificial nesting structures, became widespread in the late nineteenth century. Such practices were fueled in part by the bird protection movement and a growing interest in nature. Many people worked to stop the slaughter of birds for feathers that embellished ladies' hats at that time. Literature associated with this movement included ways to protect birds by offering them food and shelter. Many books were dedicated to attracting "bird neighbors." Around the same time, the introduction of cameras and early binoculars allowed people to study birds without killing them.

Notable government publications from the U. S. Bureau of Biological Survey focused on making homes for birds. In biologist Ned Dearborn's *Farmer's Bulletin No. 609* (1914), he states, ". . . no attraction for summer birds is more effectual than a series of houses suited to the needs and habits of the various kinds of house birds." Dearborn then outlined various nest box designs, called "House Plans," including gourds and houses for Purple Martins, nesting shelves, bluebird, flicker, and "sparrow hawk" houses. In 1925, E. R. Kalmbach and W. L. McAtee wrote *Farmer's Bulletin No. 1456: Homes for Birds*. Some designs were again included, but this publication contained much more information about predators, in a section called *Protection Against Enemies*. By this time, the European Starling had been added to the list of such "enemies."

The nest box idea caught on, especially as a way to help bluebirds. In the 1930s, Thomas Edgar Musselman, a Quincy, Illinois-based educator and naturalist, first called attention to bluebird declines. While working at his family's business college, after having studied natural

CHIMNEY SWIFT HEROINE, AHEAD OF HER TIME

Nearly a century ago Althea Rosina Sherman became the first person to build a Chimney Swift tower and the first human ever to witness and document the birds' entire nesting cycle. Sherman had thought about building such a tower for years, but this vision did not become a reality until she was sixty-two years old. In 1915, a Chimney Swift tower of her own design was built at her home in National, Iowa. A staircase wound up and around all four floors of the chimney; small windows allowed her to peek in on the birds without frightening them. By studying living birds, Sherman broke ranks with the researchers of the day, most of whom studied dead birds. She kept meticulous notes on her observations within the twenty-eight-foot-high tower from 1918 to 1936. Her findings were published posthumously in *Birds of an*

Iowa Dooryard (1952) in the chapter, "The Home Life of the Chimney Swift."

In 2009 a group called Friends of the Sherman Swift Tower finished building a historically accurate replica of Sherman's tower near her gravesite in Garnavillo, Iowa. By the summer of 2012, Chimney Swifts were once again raising their young inside a Sherman-designed tower.

Sherman's original Chimney Swift tower eventually fell into disrepair and was about to be torn down. In 1992, it was rescued and moved to Iowa City. The Althea R. Sherman Project (althearsherman.org) began restoration on the tower in March 2013. Plans for the site include a bird sanctuary, museum, and environmental education center.

Althea Sherman (third from left) teaches neighbors about Chimney Swifts. Her Chimney Swift tower, pictured in the background, was made from pine, white oak, and native cottonwood. This twenty-eight-foot-tall, nine-foot-square wooden tower enclosed a two-foot-square artificial chimney, which protruded through the roof. © *Althea R. Sherman Collection, the Althea R. Sherman Project*

BLUEBIRD HERO

As a Minnesota teenager, Lawrence Zeleny was captivated by bluebirds, which he envisioned as "symbols of love, hope, and happiness." Accounts of his bluebird observations began to appear in bird-related journals. Although he later became a biochemist, his passion for bluebirds remained. By the late 1970s, the U.S. Fish and Wildlife Service considered Eastern Bluebirds "rare" throughout much of their original range. In 1976, the now-retired "Dr. Z" wrote a book called *The Bluebird: How You Can Help Its Fight for Survival*, followed by an article in *National Geographic* magazine. The response to this article, and the belief that research would help address bluebird conservation issues, lead Zeleny to found the North American Bluebird Society (NABS) in 1978. Zeleny, along with his wife, Olive, dedicated the remainder of his life to providing nest boxes, managing his own bluebird trail in Maryland, and tirelessly promoting bluebirds. After retiring as NABS president, Zeleny continued to serve as the group's "bluebird guru," until his death in 1995 at the age of ninety-one. Today, the North American Bluebird Society has grown to be a strong conservation voice, not only for bluebirds but also for all native cavity-nesting birds.

history at the University of Illinois, he noticed a paucity of local bluebirds. His observations led him to conclude that bluebirds simply had insufficient places to nest—fewer cavities in wooden fence posts or trees and more competition for these fewer sites from House Sparrows and European Starlings. During the 1930s, using a downy woodpecker cavity as his model, he built nearly 100 experimental bluebird nest boxes of many shapes and sizes, placing them on trees and fence posts along county roads and highways. He called his route a "trail." Eventually he set up as many as 1,000 nest boxes around his hometown. In a 1934 article in *Bird-Lore* magazine, which gained considerable attention, Musselman advocated for the establishment of bluebird trails throughout the country. Lawrence Zeleny, founder of the North American Bluebird Society, credited Musselman with being the "originator of the bluebird conservation movement."

The Wood Duck was another bird helped by the use of nest boxes. In the early 1900s, it was on the brink of extinction. By 1937,

there were active government efforts to increase populations, including one involving nest boxes. In that year, nearly 500 bark-covered wooden boxes were set up by the U.S. Bureau of Biological Survey (now the U.S. Fish and Wildlife Service) in central Illinois's Chautauqua National Wildlife Refuge. To test the wildlife management potential of nest box use for Wood Duck recovery, over the next several years biologist Art Hawkins and ornithologist Frank Bellrose made nearly 700 more Wood Duck nest boxes out of rough-cut cypress and placed them across Illinois. Wood Ducks nested in half the nest boxes—an encouraging sign. Hawkins and Bellrose would later be credited with providing the research that was largely responsible for restoring Wood Duck populations.

These are but a few examples of how nest boxes and artificial nesting structures have been developed and promoted for conservation purposes throughout the years. Designing, experimenting, testing, studying, and building for birds all continue today.

The *Audubon Birdhouse Book* contains detailed accounts on selected bird species, designs for nest boxes and other nesting structures from dedicated people who work directly with the birds, plus step-by-step building instructions. All but one of the designs have been field-tested by many, many birds. Still being trialed is a wooden version of a popular and successful PVC chickadee nest box used to help study chickadee biology for many years. It was designed by Chris Willett, the woodworker who has been involved with this book. Some of the featured nest boxes attract a host of different species, not just the one for which it is named. A "bluebird nest box" can also be used by wrens, chickadees, swallows, titmice, or flycatchers. Wood Duck nest boxes can also become Hooded Merganser nest boxes. And the list goes on.

Human-built structures have become critical to the survival of some bird species, including several cited in the *Audubon Birdhouse Book*. Chimney Swifts and Purple Martins fit into this category. For these birds particularly, humans bear a responsibility not only to provide proper housing but also to teach young people about these birds, ensuring that Chimney Swifts, Purple Martins, and other

WOODWORKING FOR BIRDS

At midlife, Bill Stovall left his pet food sales job and moved to a small cabin on Michigan's Fair Lake. There he set up a woodshop and, with the encouragement and designs of ornithologist friend Dick Schinkel, started making nest boxes. At the time, in the mid-1980s, many commercial bird homes weren't built with bird safety in mind. "Things I found on the market were stapled together," recalls Stovall. "I wanted to be a good-quality manufacturer."

At first, Stovall distributed the homes himself throughout the Great Lakes region. Today, Wild Bird Centers of America and Wild Birds Unlimited, as well as lawn and garden centers nationwide, sell nest boxes and bat boxes made by Stovall Products (stovallproducts.com). The birdhouses—made from western red and northern white cedar—are still made in his own Michigan backyard by a staff of eight.

A lifelong birdwatcher, Stovall recalls making his first birdhouse from plans found in *Boy's Life* magazine. At Michigan State University and elsewhere, he and his wife, Pat, regularly host workshops about the needs of breeding birds. Stovall outlines some basics: "First, don't cut down old trees. Second, birds need healthy habitat, sources of water, and a safe environment to raise their young. Third, let's make it safe for the birds."

Bill Stovall, founder of Stovall Products, teaches a grandparents' workshop at the Pierce Cedar Creek Institute in Hastings, Michigan. *Pat Stovall*

birds will be part of their future. Other species presented here, such as owls and bluebirds, all benefit on a local level from safe and well-placed human-provided "homes."

More important, the *Audubon Birdhouse Book* covers essential "best practices" for establishing safe and dependable bird housing, including placement in the right habitats, protection from predators, proper mounting of nest boxes and artificial platforms, and maintenance of bird homes throughout the year. Vital to being a responsible "birdhouse" landlord in the twenty-first century is regularly checking in on the tenants to see how they're doing. Keeping watch over the birds that choose to live in your nest box, or on another nesting site you have provided, is a commitment that puts you in the good company of those working for bird conservation. Your efforts will pay off in beauty, perhaps even insect control, and most important, the knowledge that you are lending birds a helping hand.

BUILD HOMES ᴛᴏ BENEFIT BIRDS

As a home builder for humans and a home builder for birds, I've learned that the basic rules apply to both sets of customers: Keep 'em high and dry.

—Chris Willett, woodworker for the Audubon Birdhouse Book

An excellent first step toward building a great nest box or creating a reliable nesting structure for birds is to figure out what constitutes a poorly designed, ill-made one. Examples are all too easy to find at stores, garage sales, and sometimes even at school and community birdhouse-building events.

A checklist of bad features—some of which may be eye-catching or even advertised as beneficial—mostly applies to nest boxes for smaller birds. It includes the following:

HEAVILY PAINTED AND LACQUERED NEST BOXES: Even though nontoxic, low-VOC paints are available, plenty of premade birdhouses on the market may contain toxic, including lead, paints. Another problem with brightly painted housing, especially dark colors, is that it can create oven-like conditions inside a nest box placed in the sun. Birds see color, but it is unclear what message colors may convey. In the wild, nesting sites are primarily brown

This Eastern Screech-Owl and its Gehlbach-designed nest box both blend into their surroundings. *Fred Gehlbach*

A Wood Duck hen, incubating within her nest box, checks out a nest-checker. *Aaron Ward, courtesy of the Maryland Wood Duck Initiative*

tree holes and ledges, not highly colored miniature human houses.

PERCHES ON NEST BOXES: Perches under entry holes allow predators, especially avian predators, to gain a foothold into the nest box and its contents. These are also used by House Sparrows to lay claim to nest boxes.

GENERIC-SIZED ENTRY HOLES: Nest box entry holes should be designed to let certain birds in and keep other kinds of birds out. Entry holes that are too large may allow predators to come into the box. Entry holes that are too small could trap birds or damage their feathers. "Feather wear" occurs when birds make frequent trips into and out of nest boxes that have entry holes with tight fits or are rough or splintery. Entry holes should be appropriately sized, smooth, and well-sanded.

SHODDY CONSTRUCTION: Nest boxes that are merely stapled together may be less expensive, but they will soon fall apart. Galvanized steel screws or exterior screws (i.e., "decking screws") are the way to go.

INCORRECT FLOOR CONSTRUCTION: Avoid removable floors, which can dump nest contents, and floors nailed flush to the sides, which allow rain into the seams. Nonremovable, one-quarter-inch minimum recessed floors are recommended.

NEST BOXES MADE FROM PAPER MILK CARTONS, PLASTIC MILK JUGS, CORRUGATED CARDBOARD, OR COFFEE CANS: The idea of recycling materials for nest boxes sounds like a good one. But many of these materials, sometimes used to make nest boxes with children, are flimsy, not insulated, easy targets for prey, and quickly saturated by rain or, in the case of plastic jugs and coffee cans, prone to overheating. They do not provide "optimum" safe shelter for birds, especially featherless chicks that can become wet and chilled and die of hypothermia.

NEST BOXES FOR WARBLERS AND GOLDFINCHES: Although the male American Goldfinch and bright, good-looking warblers

These rustic bird homes could do birds more harm than good. The "porch perches" invite predators. The roof construction invites rain. They are stapled together.

do make for colorful advertising, these birds are not cavity nesters and do not use nest boxes. Steer clear of nest boxes "designed" for them.

Often the most bedazzling birdhouses for sale are the most dangerous for birds. Especially hazardous may be artistically crafted birdhouses that resemble miniature human homes. Buying a birdhouse as a work of art is fine. But enjoy this object inside your home. Do not put it outside for wild birds.

HOMEBUILDING BASICS

Generally speaking, wood remains the best building material to use for nest boxes. It keeps birds insulated from heat and cold extremes and severe weather and substitutes for the sheltering wood of tree cavities. Certain wood types and thicknesses are recommended above others. Natural gourds that are solid and mature can provide durable housing. In some cases, recycled plastic polyethylene can make a suitable nest box as well.

NEST BOX WOODS: Cedar, cypress, pine, reclaimed barn wood, and newer, less-toxic exterior grades of nonpressure-treated plywood are all recommended woods.

Western red cedar and cypress are rot- and insect-resistant. They don't need painting or staining. One drawback to cedar is that it is very soft and is easily "remodeled" by squirrels, especially at entry holes. A welcome recent development is that plywood manufacturers now offer "greener" forms of exterior plywood. The woods used for nest boxes featured in the *Audubon Birdhouse Book* are cypress, white pine, and nonpressure-treated CDX exterior grade plywood.

Wood should be at least three-quarter-inch thick. This can be confusing when purchasing wood because board references are traditional—and inaccurate. Typically wood is sold as "one-by" boards. But a one-inch (thick) by four-inch (wide) board is in reality three-quarters inch thick and three and a half inches wide.

Fortunately, three-quarter-inch thick pieces of lumber are ideal for building nest boxes.

Exterior plywood comes in varying sizes. Recommended plywood thickness for nest boxes is three-quarter inch or at least twenty-three thirty-seconds of an inch. The latter measurement is often used for plywood.

TOOLS: Nest boxes are usually simple projects, using few tools. A general list includes the following items recommended by woodworker Chris Willett:

- Eye and ear protection
- Dust mask (some dust can be toxic)
- Saws (table saw)
- Hammer
- Various screwdrivers
- Small carpenter's square or T-square
- Electric drill (cordless)
- Drill bits (assorted)
- Impact driver (cordless)
- Tape measure
- Pencil
- Clamps
- Sand paper (orbital sander)
- Wire cutters (for working with screening or hardware cloth)

Willett's references to specific tools he used to create certain nest boxes can be found in Chapter 3. Become familiar with woodworking safety rules and follow them every time.

FASTENERS: Galvanized screws such as exterior-grade deck screws are recommended for nest boxes.

Nails can be used, but only the ring-shanked, spiral, or cement-coated varieties. Two-inch (6d) nails are advised.

Common nails should not be used. They can split wood or back out over time. Brad nails and staples should never be used as the main fasteners in a nest box.

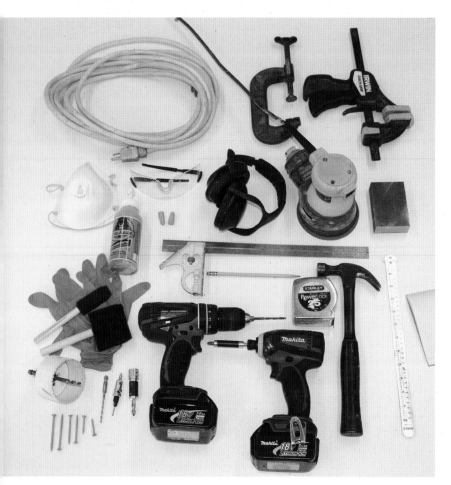

An assembly of tools and other items used by woodworker Chris Willett to make nest boxes for the *Audubon Birdhouse Book*. Chris Willett

HINGES, DOOR PIVOTS, AND CLOSURE NAILS: Several nest boxes featured in this book use hinges on nest box access doors or panels. Others use galvanized screws to serve as door pivots. For most of the nest boxes, Willett's "closure nail," which keeps the nest box securely closed between nest checks and cleaning, is a galvanized finish nail, bent about one-half inch at the head into an L shape. This allows people to open nest box doors in the field by simply pulling the nail partly out. To close things up, push the nail back into its hole. No tools required. Some paint the closure nail head a bright color, or attach it with wire or string to the nest box to avoid losing it.

CAULKS AND GLUES: Weather-resistant latex or painter's caulk is used for the inner roof of the Xbox. Some urethane-based Gorilla Glue is used on the Barn Owl nest box.

FINISHES: Nest box roofs are particularly vulnerable to wear and tear and deterioration. They will last longer if sealed and finished. Modern low-VOC semi-transparent deck stains are good choices. One such stain was used to cover Dick Tuttle's Raptor On! Kestrel nest box. Plywood should be stained to increase its durability; however, only use light colors that blend into the surroundings. In areas prone to extreme heat, very light colors, including whites used traditionally for Purple Martin housing, can help reduce the heat. A 2011 Texas Bluebird Society study showed that as nest boxes darken with age, interior temperatures can increase. The society now recommends painting darkened nest boxes exposed to hot temperatures with white or light-colored paint.

One rule applies to every nest box: If finishes are used, use them *only* on the nest box exterior. Never use paints or other finishes

Above: Improperly placed under tree branches, this Wood Duck nest box became an invitation to squirrels, not ducks. *Aaron Ward, Maryland Wood Duck Initiative*

Left: This kestrel nest box hangs on a freestanding pole; a winch will bring it safely to the ground for nest checking and cleaning. This nest box is located in great kestrel habitat: wide-open views all around, perches galore, and plenty of space to hunt. *Richard M. Tuttle*

on the insides of nest boxes. Birds that live in nest boxes deserve a nontoxic home.

NECESSARY FEATURES: Nest boxes should have the following features:

Proper ventilation: Good ventilation is essential to maintaining a dry nest box and to

The low, pole-mounted technique for Wood Duck nest boxes, coupled with the use of effective cone predator guards . . . keeps the hens safe from climbing mammalian predators, and as an important benefit, allows students to safely follow the nesting cycle—no ladders needed!

—Roger Strand, executive director of the Wood Duck Society

STEVE GILBERTSON: THINKING DIFFERENTLY FOR THE BIRDS

Much to the delight of some avian "landlords," there is a simple, effective way to mount light- to medium-weight nest boxes. Called the "Gilbertson pole-mounting system," its modest Minnesota designer, Steve Gilbertson, says he was moved to figure out how to stop raccoons from preying on his bluebirds at night. Eventually he came up with the idea of mounting a nest box on its own pole—a slick and skinny pole at that. The system is constructed of a five-foot section of half-inch conduit (a metallic tube). A similar length of half-inch rebar is attached to the conduit end with a coupler and hammered into the ground as an anchor. Gilbertson calls the system, "simple, easy, and cheap." It doesn't rust. It doesn't need cones and baffles. But it does do the job of keeping climbing predators away from nest boxes. There is some evidence it might help thwart snakes, too. Gilbertson recommends cleaning the pole with steel wool at the start of every breeding season and then spraying it, just once each season, with "cheap furniture polish—but never grease!" Gilbertson, a friend and protégé of the late bluebird champion Dick Peterson, says he was always impressed with Peterson's compassion for birds and his dedication to figuring out better ways to help them. Admirers of Gilbertson—who also invented the Gilwood nest box and the Gilbertson PVC nest box—say the same thing about him. The designers of the bluebird Xbox recommend using the Gilbertson pole system. Keith Radel of the Minnesota Bluebird Recovery Group says Gilbertson and his pole system have changed everything for the better for the birds.

A step-by-step tutorial on the Gilbertson pole mounting system is available at nestboxbuilder.com/pdf/ConduitRebar.pdf. See a photo of the Xbox mounted on a Gilbertson pole system on page 56.

prevent the heat from accumulating in the nest box in the hotter months. Entry holes provide some ventilation, but extra ventilation holes or slots are sometimes needed to keep moisture and heat away. The need for ventilation varies depending on regional differences and even day-to-day weather conditions. To avoid cold and rain, some northern nest box landlords use no ventilation holes, or very small ones, especially for nest boxes that may get used in early spring. Keeping birds warm and dry is a top priority. Nest box landlords in southern states may increase the size and number of vent holes as needed over the course of the breeding season and hot summer days. Some people drill vent holes into their nest boxes but plug them with items like wine corks or weather-stripping putty until the vents are needed. Others drill holes at an upward angle to keep rain from blowing in.

Drainage holes: There are differing opinions about the need for drainage holes. The bluebird Xbox, for example, does not have drainage holes in the plans because designers say its protective inner roof makes them unnecessary. Keeping with Willett's advice to "keep 'em high and dry," drainage holes may be necessary for many other nest box designs. Drill holes at the four corners of the nest box floor. Alternatively, woodworkers simply can cut off all four corners of the floor by three-eighths to five-eighths inch.

Easy access: Nests need to be checked and nest boxes need to be cleaned. Make sure nest boxes have at least one good way to peek inside and tidy things up. Side or front openings are typical. Some nest box plans featured in the *Audubon Birdhouse Book* show top openings. Whether a "door" pivots or hinges on the top, bottom, or side of a panel is a matter of preference. Whichever way a nest box door opens, however, it should do so in a manner that keeps bird residents most protected. The Xbox opens on the front and pivots outward from the bottom.

Overhanging roof: Ideally, roofs should overhang at least two inches in the front and one inch to two inches on the sides. Not only does this keep out water, but it provides shade too.

SETTING UP AND SETTLING IN

A well-built nest box won't do the intended bird residents any good if it is improperly placed. In fact, it could do them harm. A good rule to follow is to locate nest boxes so that food, water, and shelter are nearby. Tom

Comfort of the North American Bluebird Society says, "Remember that food is a bird's first criteria. They nest near their source of food." But different species have different food and habitat needs, and it is important for the health and safety of the birds to know what those are. For example, Purple Martins need a ready supply of flying insects; Wood Ducks require a nearby body of water; Burrowing Owls depend on premade tunnels for their nesting burrows.

Care should be taken to observe sun and shade during certain times of the day and locate nest boxes appropriately. Note which direction bad weather arrives from, then make sure nest box entry holes are not aimed that way. Keep nest boxes away from overhanging trees and places that give pests and predators—including squirrels that prey on bird eggs—easy access to the nest site. Mount nest boxes at levels where they can easily and regularly be checked. Mounting methods are discussed later in this chapter.

Nest boxes and nesting sites for certain birds may not be complete without adding nesting materials such as white pine wood chips (found in pet stores as small animal bedding) to nest boxes or adding nesting sticks to platforms. Other birds may appreciate bowls of pine needles or feathers with which to line their nests. Muddy sites close by are welcomed by several bird species, including Barn Swallows. Find out which species require which materials to help them settle in.

KEEPING THEM SAFE
PREDATOR GUARDS

Opinions and methods vary on the best ways to keep birds safe. Experimentation is ongoing, especially by those in the field. A variety of both homemade and commercially available predator guards can be used to deter both snakes and mammalian predators such as cats and raccoons. On poles or trees, metal cone baffles, cylindrical stovepipe baffles, and metal flashing can be quite effective, as is the Gilbertson pole system. One good option for nest box entry holes is the Hutchings' predator guard.

CATS

Some of the same methods used to thwart raccoons will work for cats, too, especially predator guards on poles and entry-hole guards, but cats do more than climb. They can jump five to six feet high on average. Once on top of a nest box, they need only put an exploratory paw into an unprotected entry hole and pull out what's inside. If cats are a problem—vanished nestlings, broken eggs, and piles of feathers are clues—some simple methods might help.

Place nest boxes higher than a cat can leap. Mount the nest box eight to ten feet high. Telescoping pole systems that can be raised and lowered will keep nesting birds out of cats' leaping range, but will also allow nest boxes to be lowered for regular nest checks.

A cone-shaped baffle at least thirty inches in diameter and placed on top of a cylindrical or stovepipe baffle might sound like overdoing things, but according to the Michigan Bluebird Society and other sources, it keeps cats from getting to a nest box.

A large overhanging and even slanted roof might make it more difficult for cats to access nest boxes.

Keep areas under nest boxes free of anything that could serve as a hiding place for cats that might "ambush" birds flying into and out of nest boxes.

INDOOR OR OUTDOOR CAT?
Outdoor Enclosures Provide a Little of Each

Throughout the years, cat owners have had just two choices of primary habitat for their feline

Cat enclosures may incorporate an outside screen door to allow the humans in and may connect to the house via a cat door, so cats can come and go as they please. Such enclosures keep both cats and birds safe from harm. CatsOnDeck.com

DON HUTCHINGS' PREDATOR GUARD

Don Hutchings knows about "smart" raccoons. About 20 years ago, one raccoon repeatedly attacked a quarter-mile-long section of his bluebird trail at night, killing adult birds in ten of the nest boxes. Hutchings had been thrilled to get his first bluebirds a few years earlier, and to see them being killed by raccoons didn't sit well with him. So he started designing and testing one device after another. In the end, he discovered that a six-inch-long "tunnel" attached to the nest box directly over the nest box entry hole worked best. That meant raccoons, whose arms stretch about six inches long, could only reach in as far as the end of the tunnel, but no farther. Bird occupants would remain safe. A six-inch-long section of PVC pipe, four inches in diameter, creates the tunnel. The "light at the end of the tunnel" comes from a species-specific entry hole drilled into the tunnel's cap. Hutchings says he's had no raccoon problems since he perfected his design, and he's gotten similar feedback from other people who use it too. Says Hutchings, "I might have figured out one way to outsmart raccoons."

Hutchings' predator guard plans are available at: nestbox-builder.com/nestbox-predator-controls.html

companions: confining them to the house or letting them roam outdoors. Many indoor cats can and do live happy lives, particularly if thoughtful owners provide a stimulating environment of toys, catnip, places to climb, scratching posts, and lots of attention. But indoor cats also require extra house cleaning and, sometimes, extra reupholstering. Come springtime, owners may find themselves at odds with cats that want to slip out the door at every opportunity.

If they succeed in escaping, besides posing threats to local bird populations, outdoor cats face serious threats themselves. Lurking around every corner are pesticides, antifreeze, and other poisons, as well as diseases, fleas, ticks, dogs, cat fights, and especially cars, all of which could make veterinary bills go up and a cat's life expectancy go down. Outdoor cats also kill small rodents. That might seem like a good thing, but their prowess eliminates a critical food source for owls and hawks.

There is a third option for cats that are as desperate to go out as you are to have them stay in. You may be able to compromise with a roofed-in outdoor enclosure. Such enclosures allow cats to experience the joys of the great outdoors without the hazards. You can make your outdoor enclosure even more appealing by furnishing it with tree limbs and stumps, ladders, tires, hanging toys, ledges to perch on, and boxes to hide in. Tarps over a screened roof can provide shade and protection from rain.

Enclosures can range from the simple—like a screened-in porch—to the sublime. The latter may be complete with live trees inside to serve as huge scratching posts. From the safety of their outdoor sanctuary, cats can monitor the dogs and squirrels outside, perch on ledges, sleep in the sun, run up and down trees or ladders, and stalk any moth or grasshopper that makes the fatal error of wandering into their realm.

SOME ASSEMBLY REQUIRED
Buy or Build Your Own Cat Enclosure

To build a basic outdoor kitty enclosure, attach six-foot-high wire fencing (available in green vinyl coating) to metal or wooden fence posts of equal height, pounded well into the ground. Unless you're adding a roof, bend the top two feet of fence at least forty-five degrees inward. People without the time or tools to construct a cat enclosure can order one. C&D Pet Products (cdpets.com) and Cats on Deck (catsondeck.com) both offer prefabricated kits for various-sized enclosures.

RACCOONS

The highly adaptable raccoon is a common predator of nest boxes and other nesting

The raccoon, one of the biggest—and smartest—of bird predators. *United States Fish and Wildlife Service*

sites. Once these dexterous mammals succeed at snatching eggs, young, or adult birds, they are likely to return to the scene for future meals. "Trained" or "educated" raccoons can destroy a bluebird trail or a backyard full of nest boxes. Such destruction was the inspiration for the Gilbertson pole-mounting system and the Hutchings predator guard featured in this chapter.

Clearly, where raccoons are abundant, some sort of control is essential for the safety of birds in nest boxes. Otherwise, nest boxes simply become "raccoon feeders." Typically, raccoons climb up to the nest box, hang on to the front or park themselves on the roof, reach into the entry hole, and start feasting. It helps to know that the reach of an adult raccoon is at least six inches. This is why overhanging roofs and entry hole guards like the Noel hardware cloth guard and the six-inch-long Hutchings predator guard make sense: They keep the nest box contents out of raccoon reach. Pole baffles, such as metal cones or stovepipes placed just under nest boxes, may keep raccoons from climbing up to the nest box in the first place. Metal flashing attached onto trees under owl nest boxes and onto utility poles under kestrel boxes can accomplish the same thing.

Stovepipe baffles that can be made to wobble make it even harder for raccoons to hold on. And very large stovepipe baffles—more than a foot in diameter or more—work even better at keeping raccoons off nest boxes. Raccoons just can't shimmy up them.

SNAKES

Snakes can pose big problems at nest boxes, especially in the southern states. Predator guards such as metal cones or stovepipes placed under nest boxes can help deter snakes, but make sure the guards fit tightly around whatever kind of pole is used. Snakes can crawl through very small spaces. The top of stovepipe guards should be blocked. One method fastens hardware cloth across the top but just inside the guard; however, studies show that snakes longer than five feet can probably make it around most any baffle.

Snake traps, such as the Krueger, are made from galvanized wire and garden netting. Trapped snakes can then be released unharmed

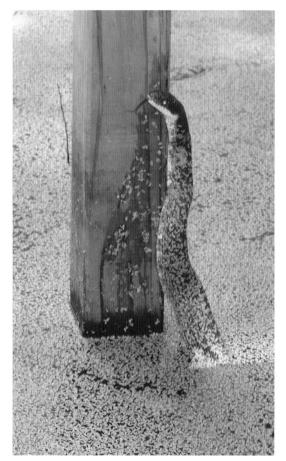

Above: Predator guards, like this metal cone guard, must fit snugly against support posts or poles. Otherwise a gap, like the one shown here, can be space enough for a snake to slip through. *Aaron Ward, courtesy of the Maryland Wood Duck Initiative*

Left: A black rat snake, covered in bright green duckweed, tries to reach a Wood Duck nest box set up on top of the post in a marsh along Maryland's eastern shore. These versatile snakes, more active at night and in summer, are excellent climbers. *Aaron Ward, courtesy of the Maryland Wood Duck Initiative*

from the mesh elsewhere. As with baffles, they are affixed just below the nest box.

EUROPEAN STARLINGS AND HOUSE SPARROWS

House Sparrows may raise two to three broods, and starlings three to four broods per year—often within a human-provided nest box. Both of these species may kill young and adult native birds and then take over their nest boxes. There are many stories about "landlords" going to check on their native nesting birds, only to find a House Sparrow nest built not only on top of

Above: A starling (top) and an Eastern Bluebird (bottom) fight over a nest box, an all-too-common sight in some areas.
David Kinneer

Right: A Sparrow Spooker, pictured here, is a normal part of these young bluebirds' new world. The fluttering Mylar streamers scare off House Sparrows but not other birds. Attaching the Sparrow Spooker after the desired bird's first egg has been laid seems to work best. Homemade for years, Sparrow Spookers are now commercially available.
David Kinneer

Avoid human populations: Nest box placement may be key. Both House Sparrows and starling populations thrive near humans. Placing a nest box far away from human habitation and known starling and House Sparrow populations might improve the chances of it being occupied by a native bird.

Members only: Another method is not to put out nest boxes until a preferred species' arrival date or breeding period, or to keep nest box entrances boarded up until that time. The idea is that House Sparrows in particular, which have year-round territories, won't be able to claim the nest box first. But it will be available when the more desirable bird shows up seeking a nest site.

Exclude them: Usually, a one-and-a-half-inch entrance hole will exclude starlings but allow Eastern Bluebirds, swallows, titmice, chickadees, and others easy passage. Unfortunately, one of those "others" are House Sparrows. They can be excluded by a one-and-a-quarter-inch entry hole; however, this protects only very small cavity nesters.

SREHS

Anyone dabbling in Purple Martin circles soon learns the acronym "SREH." It stands for "starling-resistant entry hole," and the device has been a valuable asset in the fight against starlings. In the late 1980s, Charles McEwen of New Brunswick, Canada, weary of starling havoc in his martin colony, began experimenting with ways to keep them out of the compartments. Working through many trials, he came up with a solution: a half-moon, crescent-shaped entry hole, three inches long and one and three-sixteenth inches high. Purple Martins can get through these holes, but starlings cannot. McEwen's design works for both martin gourds and houses; crescent-shaped adapters can be placed over older-style entry holes. Purple Martin landlord Chuck Abare of Alabama reports that SREHs come with a bonus. Not only do they work to foil starlings, but they also keep out jays, crows, owls, gulls, squirrels, and raccoons, which also attack martins. "SREHs have completely changed my Purple Martin colony," says Abare. "It is now starling free." For his contributions, the Purple Martin Conservation Association named Charles McEwen "Landlord of the Year" in1992.

a native bird's nest but on top of the victims themselves. Discovering such events can be disturbing and heartbreaking but can also provide the inspiration to take back control from the more aggressive sparrows and starlings.

Over the years, the idea of both "passive" and "active" control for nonnative starlings and House Sparrows has come into play.

PASSIVE CONTROL

Passive controls involve ways to outsmart House Sparrows and starlings without removing them. Some passive methods follow:

Move the nest box: If a nest box is up and starlings or House Sparrows take over, move it somewhere else. Many people have success with this simple method; however, some point out that this "rule" also limits the chances of native birds nesting in a particular area.

Multiple layers of House Sparrow nests built over time fill this bluebird nest box. House Sparrow nests are bulky balls of grasses, human detritus, and seed heads, lined with feathers, hair, and string. Even when nests are removed, the male House Sparrow may be relentless in his efforts to reclaim the nesting site.
Bet Zimmerman, sialis.org

A male House Wren has built a "dummy" nest of sticks on top of an Eastern Bluebird's nest. The bluebirds have departed, and the dummy nest has no eggs.
Bet Zimmerman, sialis.org

ACTIVE CONTROL

Sometimes sparrow and starling populations are so high, and the birds so aggressive against native species, active control may be the most realistic way to reduce their numbers and give cavity-nesting birds a chance to reproduce.

Because starlings and House Sparrows are not protected under the Migratory Bird Treaty Act, it is legal to remove their nests and eggs. The male House Sparrow, bonded more to a nest site than to his mate, often begins rebuilding a nest immediately. Although the adults may eventually move—and try to oust other native birds from nesting sites elsewhere—continuous nest removal may discourage the birds and result in them giving up a claimed nest box.

Ironically, in recent years, both House Sparrows and European Starlings have been listed as threatened in the United Kingdom from where they were first imported to North America. Because these two native U.K. "garden birds" have declined dramatically, conservation plans are in effect to help restore their populations. Exactly why these bird numbers have dropped is a mystery; however, it is known that House Sparrows have suffered from a shortage of insects during breeding months, especially in urban areas like London. Starlings have been affected by the loss of old meadows.

HOUSE WRENS: OCCASIONAL HOME WRECKERS

The beautiful song of the House Wren may not seem so beautiful after it has ransacked a nest box, destroying eggs by puncturing them. A pile of sticks on top of the victim's nest is another telltale sign the House Wren has visited. Proper nest box placement may prevent

A hornet nest takes over a Wood Duck nest box. *Aaron Ward, Maryland Wood Duck Initiative*

Blowfly larvae are common in many nest boxes. The female blowfly lays eggs in bird nests. The larvae then attach to the soft parts of young birds, feeding mostly at night. In large enough numbers, they can harm and even kill nestlings. *Bet Zimmerman, sialis.org*

this havoc. Keep nest boxes far away from brushy areas that wrens seem to prefer. Another preventative measure is to install an Orthwein wren guard. The late Bob Orthwein invented a simple guard to block wrens' views of nest box entry holes. A thin, L-shaped piece of wood as wide as the box, is tacked onto the front edge of the roof, hanging down a few inches so it covers sight of the entry hole. A space of two to three inches between the guard and the entry hole allows nest box birds to enter and leave. Variations have since been created, but the

concept is the same: out of wren sight, out of wren mind. Guards should be attached when native birds have laid a first egg but removed a few days before young birds fledge.

SIX-LEGGED NEST BOX PESTS
Blowfly larvae
Adult blowflies lay their eggs in nest boxes, and their larvae feast on young birds, usually attaching to soft parts like the face and feet. One action to take is to install a simple three-eighths-inch square hardware cloth blowfly trap. Bend wire about one inch from each end to create a kind of table so the trap covers the entire nest box floor. The nest is lifted slightly off the floor, allowing blowfly larvae to fall underneath during daylight when they move away from the light that enters the box. They can then be cleaned out easily. Designed by the late Ira Campbell of Virginia.

Paper wasps
Both native and more aggressive European paper wasps build nests in nest boxes and under baffles, but they can be dissuaded. Before birds return to nest, rub the ceiling and inner walls of the nest box with unscented Ivory or Fels-Naptha soap. If birds are present, temporarily cover the nests while "soaping" the insides. Birds may abandon nests if wasps are inside the nest box. Because wasps can make nests under nest boxes and inside predator guards, approach these areas with caution.

Gnats, black flies, and more
Black flies, also called buffalo gnats, kill nestlings by feeding on them, causing anemia or shock. Remedies are few and unproven. Some people spray vanilla or mouthwash around nest boxes as a nontoxic pesticide-free way to ward them off. Fortunately, black flies usually are only active for a few weeks in spring

Interacting with my martins by doing nest checks, keeping invasive sparrows and starlings under control, and just simply being around the birds has helped immensely in growing my colony. Purple Martins are people lovers and I've got over one hundred pairs to prove it!

—*Chuck Abare, designer of Chuck's Simple Wooden Gourd Rack Design*

> Building a nest box and putting it up is the easy part. Monitoring and maintaining nest boxes over the years is the hard part. But really, it's the most important work you'll do.
>
> —*Steve Simmons, designer of the Barn Owl nest box*

Other pests can infest nest boxes, too, including ants, bees, yellow jackets, hornets, and even queen bumblebees. Fire ants are a particular problem in southern states. Small insects, such as lice and fleas, and arachnids, such as mites and ticks, may infect and live on bird hosts. Never use insecticides to control the pests, as birds will suffer.

CHECKING IN

As the late bluebird hero Dick Peterson advised, "Weekly nest checks tell you everything." It is recommended that those who put up nest boxes or artificial nesting structures check in with nesting birds at least once a week during the breeding season to see how they are getting along. Nest checks—as simple as a quick peek into the nest—can reveal birds in trouble. Aim to make these checks last less than a minute—half a minute if you can—and deal with problems quickly. Many problems are easy to solve. Nest-checking affords a good way to get to know the birds you are giving homes.

Some general rules to follow are provided by the Cornell Lab of Ornithology's NestWatch program:

Look around for potential nest predators, such as crows, blue jays, and house cats, before approaching active nests. These predators can easily learn from you where to find a snack. If predators are present, it is best to delay the nest check until another time.

Do not check early in the morning. Most female birds lay their eggs in the morning. Also, because parent birds usually leave the nest during a check, on cold mornings, their untended eggs and nestlings can become cold quickly.

Avoid nest checks during the first days of incubation.

Avoid nest checks during bad weather. If the day is cold, damp or rainy, postpone the check until another day.

Above: Sometimes, nest checks reveal unexpected birds and unexpected beauty. This Tree Swallow is nesting in a bluebird nest box, its lovely nest lined with feathers that curl over the eggs. *Bet Zimmerman*

This Wood Duck nest box is easy to open and to check, a requirement for any nest box. *Aaron Ward, Maryland Wood Duck Initiative*

Bluebirder Bet Zimmerman checks a Gilfort bluebird nest box, quickly and quietly. *Doug Zimmerman, sialis.org*

A male bluebird (left) watches over his seventeen-day-old chick as it takes its first flight. *David Kinneer*

Do not check nests around or after dusk, when parents are returning to the nests for the night. Owls are the exception to this rule; owl parents leave their nests at dusk.

Do not approach nests when young are close to fledging. Disturbances can make the birds fledge early. That is when they are most likely to fall victim to predators. If you are unsure of the average fledge date, a good rule to follow is to stop nest checks ten days after hatching.

Avoid handling healthy nests, eggs, and nestlings—all are fragile and all are protected by law. In addition, eggs touched by humans may pick up oil and make them less porous.

Basic tools for nest checking include plastic bags, rubber or leather gloves, and a tool like a trowel, spatula, or putty knife. Clothes with deep pockets or an apron to hold all these items will keep your hands free. Wear a good hat. Some people use a mechanic's mirror to help see inside nest boxes.

It is best to wait for adult birds to leave before checking in on the nest. Wood Duck hens make things easy. They seem to have regular times, twice a day, when they leave the nest to forage. If it is unclear if adults are present, walk toward the nest box making slight sounds to alert any birds inside, then stand to the side of the nest box and rap lightly on the front panel. Birds that are still inside will often fly out. Then, proceed to slowly open the nest

box before peeking in. When done, walk away quickly. On occasion, nest boxes can hold surprises, like snakes or stinging insects.

A mental checklist can be helpful: Are there signs that predators have visited? Are there unhatched eggs, dead chicks, or dead adults that need to be removed? Their prompt removal prevents them from attracting pests and predators and creating unsanitary conditions. Are young birds tangled in nesting materials like strings or plastic fishing lines? Any indications of invading starlings or House Sparrows? Do you see small pests or parasites? Anything unusual at all? Nest boxes and nesting structures can age, sometimes less than gracefully. Do repairs need to be made? If the answers are all negative, all may be well.

Nest checkers want to avoid frightening or stressing the birds. Bluebirder Bet Zimmerman points out that different species seem to have different tolerance levels for humans. Bluebirds and Tree Swallows seem to be nonplussed by checks. Many females even remain on their eggs during nest checks, but birds like titmice may be more timid.

Remain calm at the nest site and try to avoid being startled by the birds themselves. Tree Swallows may fly close to a checker as a way to protect their nest, but that's about all they'll do. Chickadees may vocalize loudly, uttering their "scold" call.

Although it is recommended to stop nest checks a few days before birds fledge—and those dates vary with the species—you can watch them at a distance. Pay special attention and with luck you might witness a priceless event: a fledgling's first flight.

Many nest checkers take notes on their birds: how many eggs, how many nestlings, signs of blowflies, and so on. Some people keep their own personal records over the years. In California, Steve Simmons' nest-checking data goes back forty years, a record that is now a valuable resource for some bird population studies. People also submit their records to the Cornell Lab of Ornithology's NestWatch program, which uses data from many nest checkers to study the nesting success and failures of breeding birds in North America.

HOUSEKEEPING

Nest boxes should be cleaned thoroughly at least once at the end of the breeding season to make the site available for birds looking for a winter roost. A cleaned-out nest box also helps control other pests and parasites. It is illegal to remove the active nest of a protected bird species—that is, a nest that is clearly in use, but you can remove the inactive nests of native birds once the nesting season is over.

For nest boxes that shelter more than one brood per season, many advocate cleaning out nests soon after young birds fledge in order to prevent parasites from affecting the next brood. Another practical reason to remove these nests is that adults might build a new nest on top of the first one. That means the next brood is closer up to the entry hole, where they could become easier pickings for predators such as raccoons.

If possible, wear rubber gloves and a mask when performing cleaning chores, to avoid contact with dust and dried feces. Use a metal

In Missouri, this Eastern Bluebird pair investigates an Xbox in February. Putting up nest boxes early in the year gives some birds an advantage. *Leisa Nesbit*

spatula, putty knife, or ice scraper to lift out the old nest. A stiff outdoor grill brush is a great tool for sweeping out bits of the nest, including the remains of old wasp nests. This is also the time to clean out any clogged drainage holes. If there were feather lice or other parasites from the previous nesting, consider disinfecting the nest box with a 10 percent chlorine-free bleach solution, sprayed inside the nest box. Then leave the nest box open to thoroughly dry.

Many people keep nest boxes up all winter to serve as roosting sites for birds. If you do, make sure to check the nest box and clean it out once again before the start of the breeding season. Even if you cleaned things out well at summer's end, mice may still have built nests in the fall. If you find mouse nests come spring, don gloves and mask, remove the grassy nest, and disinfect once again. Then you are ready for the new nesting season to begin.

Construct a safe, dry environment for birds; mount nest boxes properly with predators in mind; and above all, take responsibility for nest box tenants. Check nest boxes throughout the nesting season. Keep watch over your birds.

—*Sherry Linn, president, North American Bluebird Association*

CHAPTER 3

BIRDS IN BOXES

GREAT NEST BOXES FOR GREAT BIRDS

Birds that take most readily to nest boxes generally fall into two groups: primary cavity nesters and secondary cavity nesters. Woodpeckers, chickadees, and nuthatches are in this first category. They chisel out and customize nesting spaces inside trees or wooden posts. In contrast, bluebirds seek out prefabricated homes, those made by primary cavity nesters or formed naturally by funguses or weather-related events.

Rotting trees suitable for excavation by the primary group have become increasingly hard for these birds to find, and ready-made nesting cavities for the secondary

Above: A Carolina Chickadee checks out an Xbox. This new and innovative bluebird nest box is a good one for chickadees, flycatchers, swallows, and titmice, too. *David Kinneer*

Right: A pair of House Finches seems to be inspecting a weathered bluebird house. House Finches are not that particular where they nest. This might make a good home for them. *David Kinneer*

This Carolina Chickadee has completed nest cavity excavation in the Francis Beidler Forest of South Carolina, an Audubon sanctuary.
Mark Musselman

group are even scarcer. Nest boxes can help fill this availability gap.

The nest box designs chosen for this book have been guided by nest sites found in the wild. They have been tested and tweaked by those experienced with using nest boxes to help birds. The plans are arranged according to build difficulty, from easy to more complex.

Nest box designs are always changing, and with good reason. These structures are inherently artificial, but ongoing research and field-testing are helping a variety of birds to accept nest boxes and behave naturally within them. And although "perfect" nest boxes do not exist, some are far safer and more effective than others. The nest boxes featured here are designed, first and foremost, with the health and safety of the birds in mind.

To "please the birds" is a good rule of thumb to follow when making nest boxes, whether you are participating in a large-scale "citizen science" project, or simply keeping tabs on your nest box guests for your own records. The following pages will provide you with information, woodworking plans, and tips to create great nest boxes for great birds.

In the Spring Valley Wildlife Area of Ohio, a female Prothonotary Warbler pauses in front of her nest site with a beakful of nesting materials. Premade dwellings such as this, chiseled out by a primary cavity nester, have become rare commodities.
Ruhikanta Meetei

WRENS

Bewick's Wren

Thryomanes bewickii

Like the Carolina Wren, Bewick's Wren has a distinctive long white eyebrow. *Ashok Khosla*

Breeding

Year-round

Wintering

Forest fragmentation and increased bird feeding in this century have benefited Carolina Wrens and House Wrens; however, Bewick's Wrens have virtually disappeared in the East and declined in the western parts of their range. The egg- and nest-destroying House Wren may be partly responsible. Wherever House Wrens have expanded, Bewick's Wrens have declined. Carolina Wrens have been wintering farther north, possibly due to climate change.

RANGE: Bewick's Wrens inhabit drier habitats in the U.S. Southwest and coastal California. It is rare and endangered in parts of its eastern range. Carolina Wrens are most common in southern states but are found throughout the eastern United States and Central America. House Wrens breed across Canada, down to the tip of South America, and into the West Indies—the broadest latitudinal range of any native songbird.

FIELD MARKS: Carolina Wrens are the largest of these wrens—about five and a half inches long with a seven-and-a-half-inch wingspan. Bewick's Wrens are slightly smaller, and House Wrens are even smaller. The light-brown, chestnut, and cinnamon coloration is similar. Bewick's and Carolina Wrens have a bold white stripe above the eyes; Bewick's has white tail spots. House Wrens lack both and are overall drabber birds. Wrens are identifiable by their distinctive habit of cocking their tails up over their backs.

VOICE: Wrens sing extremely varied songs, filled with churrs, buzzes, rattles, and bubbling liquid trills. Carolina Wrens sing a clear, three-syllabled *tea-kettle, tea-kettle, tea-kettle*. Bewick's Wrens also have a three-part song. House wren song is described as "long and bubbly." All three species utter harsh "scold" notes.

FEEDING: These small insectivores eat beetles, cotton-boll weevils, stink bugs, leafhoppers, scale insects, crickets, millipedes, snails, sow bugs, and grasshoppers, as well as occasional lizards and fruits. Carolina Wrens may visit bird feeders.

Carolina Wren

Thryothorus ludovicianus

The Carolina Wren sings *tea-kettle, tea-kettle, tea-kettle.*
David Kinneer

This Carolina Wren demonstrates the tail-up pose characteristic of all wrens.
David Kinneer

Year-round

House Wren

Troglodytes aedon

Despite its small size, the House Wren can be aggressive toward many other species during the nesting season, including bluebirds.
Ashok Khosla

Breeding

Year-round

Wintering

THE NEST SITE

The wrens' insect-eating habits make them friends of gardeners. Build a brush pile in a backyard corner to attract insects for them. Plant pines, bayberries, and sweet gum. Because of House Wrens' destructive habits, put up standard wren houses for Bewick's Wrens *only* where House Wrens are rare or absent. Remove House Wren nest boxes during nonbreeding seasons. Wren houses for Bewick's and House Wrens can be found at the following website, courtesy of the Northern Prairie Wildlife Research Center: npwrc.usgs.gov/resource/wildlife/ndblinds/ndblinds.pdf.

NESTING: Wrens nest in tree cavities and upturned tree roots but also in an odd assortment of human-provided housing, including flowerpots, mailboxes, and even trouser pockets on clotheslines. Bewick's Wrens construct a nest of leaves, sticks, and spider-egg cases, lined with feathers, wool, and plant down. The Carolina Wren's bulky nest consists of grass, bark, leaves, moss, feathers, and snakeskin. House Wrens make multiple "dummy" nests, filling entire nest cavities with sticks.

- EGGS: Range from four to eight, but usually five white eggs with rusty brown spots. Bewick's eggs are paler overall.
- EGG-LAYING: One egg per day.
- INCUBATION: Twelve to fourteen days. Female incubates; both parents feed young.
- DAYS TO FLEDGE: Twelve to fourteen days.

PLACING THE NEST BOX: Carolina Wrens frequent backyard gardens with dense shrubs and forested areas with underbrush and fallen trees, especially near water. Place their nest boxes in protected areas, especially under overhanging roofs. Both Bewick's and House Wrens nest just about anywhere, even in old boots, buckets, and flower pots. Keep House Wren nest boxes far away from other nesting birds.

- MOUNTING: Use nails, screws, rope, or wire to secure the Orthwein nest box within a sheltered place.
- HEIGHT: Place the Orthwein nest box and other wren nest boxes five to ten feet high.

BEHIND THE DESIGN

The late Bob Orthwein of Ohio is perhaps best known in bluebird circles for his wren guards. He also designed nest boxes, including one for Carolina Wrens. He had observed Carolina Wren nests ". . . under roofs of open porches, open barns, or open sheds"—places that obliged the bird to fly in and *then* up to the nest site. With these clues, Orthwein went to work designing a comfortable, simple-to-make shelter that was easier for the birds to fly directly into. In winter 1997, his Carolina Wren nest box plans were unveiled in a cheerily titled article written for the Ohio Bluebird Society's newsletter: *Finally, Carolina Wrens!*

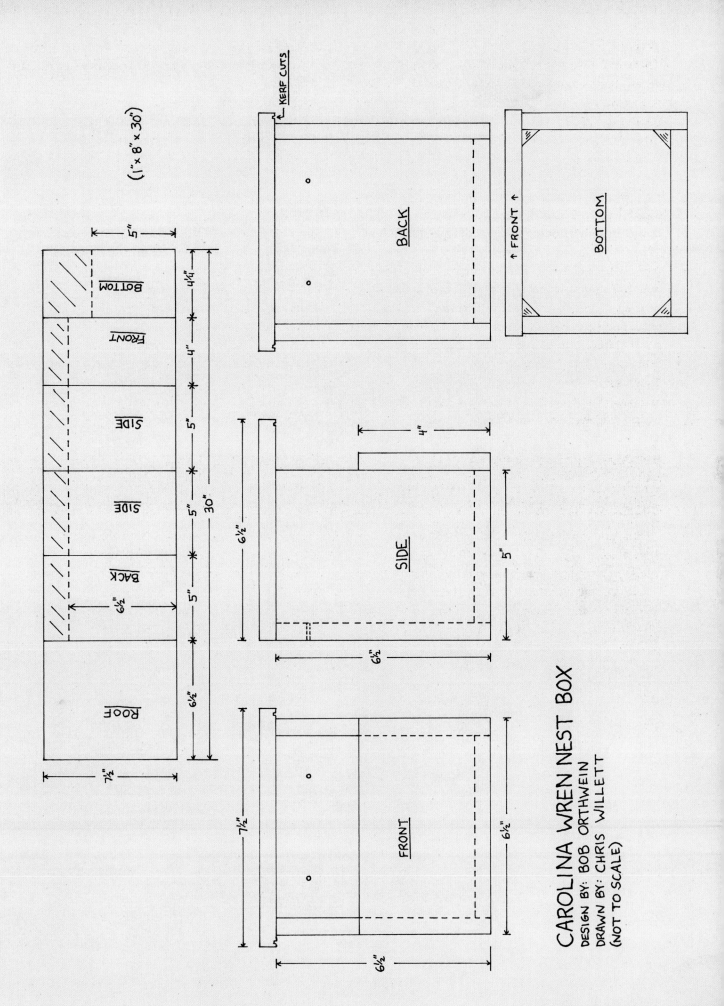

CAROLINA WREN NEST BOX

DESIGN BY: BOB ORTHWEIN
DRAWN BY: CHRIS WILLETT
(NOT TO SCALE)

CAROLINA WREN NEST BOX

DESIGNED BY BOB ORTHWEIN

MATERIALS

- 1x8x30" cypress (used here) or cedar (actual size is ¾" thick x 7 ½" wide)
- Fourteen to eighteen 2" exterior grade decking screws

1

Cut pieces out according to the drawings. Make kerf cuts on the underside of the roof piece (⅜" in from edge and ¼" deep), along the front and two sides. These shallow grooves, used in many nest box plans, are usually made with a table saw. They help prevent rainwater from collecting underneath the roof and getting inside the nest box.

2

Cut approximately ¾" off each corner of the floor piece to create drainage holes.

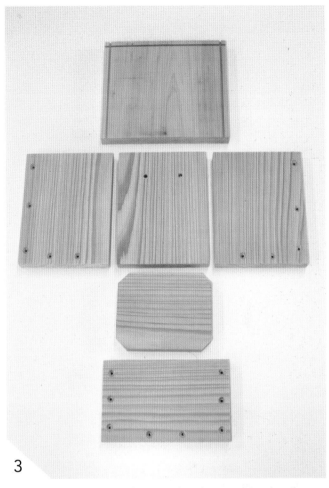

3

Assemble the pieces. The front panel can be secured with as few as four screws.

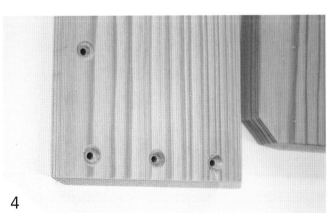

4

Predrilling is recommended to avoid splitting the wood.

5

Recess the floor piece slightly to help keep the floor dry. Secure sides to floor, then front to the sides. Drill out the mounting screw hole locations. Hang the Carolina Wren box under roofs or eaves.

Prothonotary Warbler

Protonotaria citrea

A male Prothonotary Warbler, with a mouthful of insects, pauses en route to the expectant chicks back at its nest box along the lower James River in Virginia. The metal band on its right leg helps researchers understand more about the bird's life history. Within its bill are a crane fly, assassin bug, caterpillar, mayfly, and two beetles. *James R. Reilly*

Breeding
Local breeding
Wintering

Female Prothonotary Warblers are slightly less colorful than males. Both have relatively long bills. *Mark Musselman*

The only eastern warblers to nest in tree cavities, these stunningly bright yellow birds—once called Golden Swamp Warblers—have declined considerably throughout their range over the past four decades. Reasons include rapidly disappearing mangrove swamp habitat in the Caribbean and in Central and South America where the birds overwinter, along with degradation and fragmentation of their breeding grounds. Prothonotary nests can also be parasitized by cowbirds.

RANGE: Abundant in woodland swamps in the southeastern United States, along the East Coast from Canada to Florida, and west into Texas, Oklahoma, and Kansas. Scattered populations exist elsewhere.

FIELD MARKS: Males are a brilliant yellow-orange on the head and breast, with blue-gray wings and a greenish back. Females are duller. Both sexes show white on the belly and under the tail. During breeding season, Prothonotaries' long, pointed bills are black; these turn paler come fall.

VOICE: The loud notes of Prothonotaries—a classic *tweet, tweet, tweet*—are sung at the same pitch.

FEEDING: Prothonotaries hop on the ground or on tree bark while foraging for insects like beetles, spiders, and caterpillars. They also visit feeders.

THE NEST SITE

Prothonotaries return from wintering areas in early spring. Though mostly insectivorous, these warblers sometimes eat feeder treats like grape jelly, suet, and hummingbird nectar. They also use birdbaths and nest boxes. The health of Prothonotary populations depends largely on the preservation of their breeding and wintering grounds.

NESTING: Prothonotaries prefer nesting in woodpecker holes near wooded swamps, but they also set up house in nest boxes, as well as odd places like sneakers, tin cans, and jacket pockets. Males build "dummy" moss nests in several different sites. The female selects one nest and finishes it with more moss, plant down, grasses, leaves, and rootlets.

- EGGS: Range from three to seven white to pinkish eggs with rusty-brown to lavender spots. Up to three broods per season.
- EGG-LAYING: One egg per day.
- INCUBATION: About two weeks.
- DAYS TO FLEDGE: About eleven days. Both parents care for young up to thirty-five days after first flight.

PLACING THE NEST BOX: Place nest boxes in shaded areas near lakes, swamps, slow-moving rivers, and thick deciduous understory. Nest boxes placed over water and kept free of brush and branches may help deter predators. If over water, face entry hole toward land. If on land, face toward water.

- MOUNTING: Place nest box on top of three-quarter-inch diameter metal conduit pole with a one-quarter-inch hole drilled near one end to accept single bolt through box and pole. Use of single bolt allows box angle to be adjusted if pole leans off vertical a bit. If in water, sink pole at least two feet into lake bottom for stability. Place ten to twenty feet away from the bank to deter predators. Include predator guards, both on land or in water.
- HEIGHT: Make sure height is convenient for nest checking, especially if checking by boat. If over water, the bottom of the nest box should be at least two feet above the highest potential water level. Allow for tidal swings.

Spring's return stirs this male Prothonotary Warbler to sing. *Mark Musselman*

BEHIND THE DESIGN

Virginia Commonwealth University (VCU) professor Bob Reilly claims that come spring, "Prothonotaries are just every-where" along the lower James River near Richmond, Virginia. Reilly supervises banding efforts for VCU's long-term study of Prothonotary Warbler breeding biology. Since the study's start in the mid-1980s, researchers have banded more than 35,000 warblers. With help from Richmond Audubon Society volunteers, more than 650 pine nest boxes are readied each year for the Prothonotaries' return. One of Reilly's key design modifications was to reduce the entry hole to one and a quarter inches, "which makes it a tight fit for cowbirds and competitive Tree Swallows." He notes that the James River birds seem wary of brand new nest boxes, preferring homes that are "plain and weathered." Even though the pine wood homes only last about five years, he adds, "We want our nest boxes to please the birds, not ourselves."

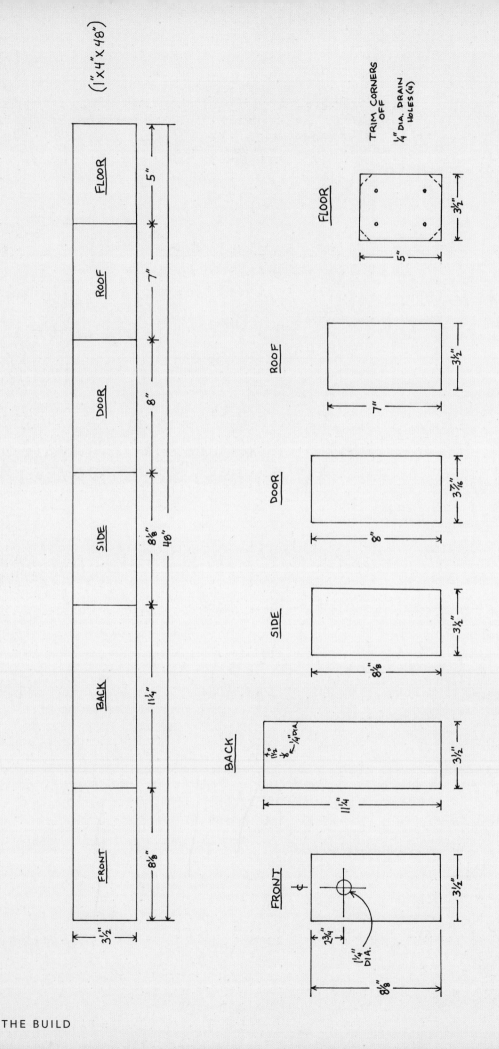

PROTHONOTARY WARBLER BOX

DESIGN BY: BOB REILLY
DRAWN BY: CHRIS WILLETT
(NOT TO SCALE)

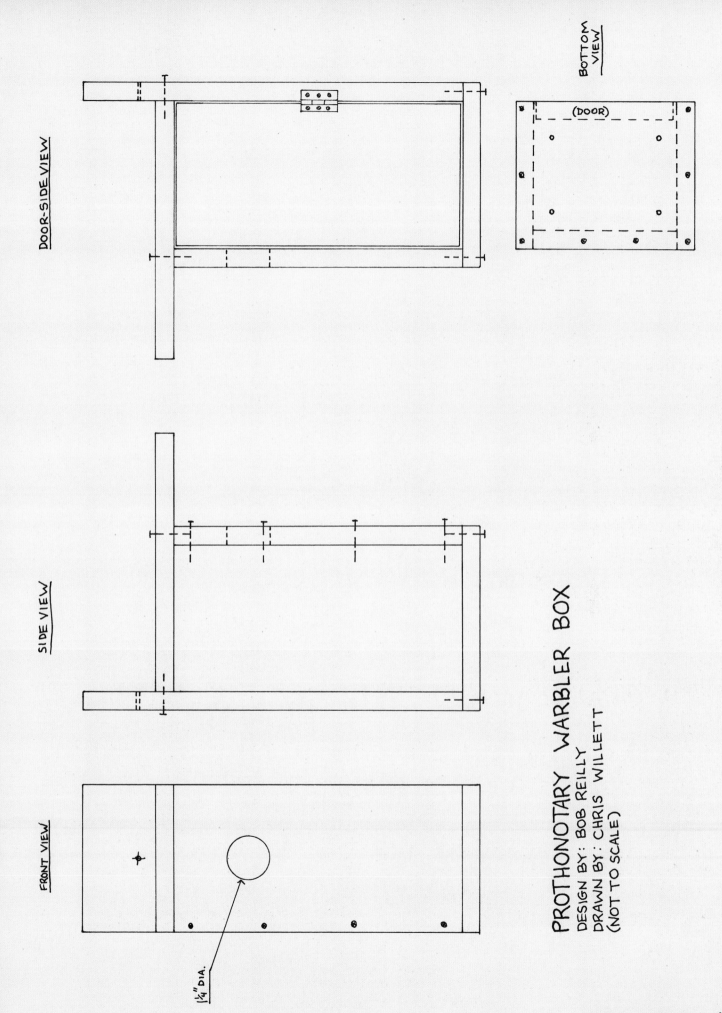

DOOR-SIDE VIEW

BOTTOM VIEW

(DOOR)

SIDE VIEW

FRONT VIEW

1¼" DIA.

PROTHONOTARY WARBLER BOX
DESIGN BY: BOB REILLY
DRAWN BY: CHRIS WILLETT
(NOT TO SCALE)

PROTHONOTARY WARBLER NEST BOX

DESIGNED BY BOB REILLY

MATERIALS

- One 1"x4"x8' cypress (used here), untreated pine, or cedar board (makes two nest boxes)
- One 1½"x1½" exterior hinge, and the ¾" screws that come with the hinges
- Eighteen 1½" exterior-grade deck screws
- One ¼"x2½" bolt, nut, and washer
- One 1¼" exterior screw (door handle)
- One 2½" galvanized nail (bent for latch nail)

1

Cut all pieces according to the drawing.

2

Drill the entrance hole 1¼" diameter with the top of the hole 1½" down on the front piece, centered side-to-side on the front piece.

3

4

Predrill all exterior screw holes with a ⅛" drill bit. Predrill hinge screw sites with a 1⁄16" drill bit. Drill hole for front piece latch nail. Attach latch nail to front piece. Drill four holes (¼") in floor for drainage. Assemble and attach all pieces except the side door.

Finally, drill the 1¼" screw into the side door to use as a door handle. Test-fit the door. Attach it to the back piece with the hinge. The side door should open freely. The finished Prothonotary Warbler nest box was bolted through the back onto a u-channel signpost (opposite page). A stovepipe baffle provides protection from predators.

QUICK TIP

Properly sized drill bits and hole saws can make precision cuts for entry holes. One way to prevent splitting when making the entry hole is to drill only halfway through the front piece. Then, flip the front over and finish the job from the other side. Always sand entry hole edges smooth.

BLUEBIRDS

Clockwise from far top left:

A female Eastern Bluebird will eat this holly berry whole. *David Kinneer*

This male Mountain Bluebird brings food to his young in a natural tree cavity. *Russ Amy*

Brightly colored Western Bluebirds (the male is pictured here) have been successfully reintroduced to the San Juan Islands, where nest boxes were provided for them. *Ashok Khosla*

In the natural world, all three species of North American bluebirds—the Eastern, Western, and Mountain Bluebirds—seek tree cavities or woodpecker holes for nesting sites. But today, natural cavities can be hard to find. Competition for these limited sites is a huge problem, especially in early spring. Old and rotting trees often are removed. Not long ago, many bluebirds nested in wooden fence posts, especially around farms. Many of those have been removed or replaced with treated wood, plastic, or metal posts. A well-built and well-placed bluebird nest box in your own backyard or nearby park can help boost local populations.

Even with nest boxes in place, bluebirds must compete with both introduced and native species that also want to call these nest boxes their home. Knowing where to place and where *not* to place bluebird nest boxes is critical. Chickadees and titmice, for example, prefer nest boxes near or under mature trees or within woodlands and forests. By contrast, bluebirds like nest boxes out in the open; even a small yard with open spaces will suit a bluebird. Most important, bluebirds need to live near a ready supply of insect food.

Since bluebirds defend large feeding territories around their nests—one or two acres in early spring—they don't want to nest close to other bluebirds. Tree Swallow pairs won't nest close to one another either. So reduce competition by installing pairs of bluebird nest boxes no more than fifteen to twenty feet apart. Bluebirds may nest in one, and swallows, chickadees, or titmice in the other. This "peaceable kingdom" occurs for practical reasons: These bird neighbors, by and large, do not share the same food supply. But the nest box "pairing" idea is not without differing opinions. Some people believe it encourages other species more than it accommodates bluebirds. Others put up a second box nearby only when a non-bluebird species has claimed a nest box first.

Ironically, the cutting of Eastern forests, especially pine woods, for agriculture in the nineteenth century may have actually benefited Eastern Bluebirds by creating additional foraging and nesting habitat. More recently, however, their populations have been affected by loss of habitat and tree cavities, unusually cold winters in the 1960s and 1970s, egg and chick predation, and competition for nesting sites by introduced House Sparrows and European Starlings.

Eastern Bluebird

Sialia sialis

This Eastern Bluebird is communicating using behavior known as "wing-waving." *David Kinneer*

Breeding

Year-round

Wintering

RANGE: Eastern Bluebirds are year-round residents in the southern United States. They typically begin nesting as early as January in the south and in March in the northern United States and southern Canada. They are also found in parts of Mexico, Central America, and Bermuda.

FIELD MARKS: Males are bright blue above and rusty orange below with a white belly. Females look similar but have a blue-gray back and lighter orange underparts. Both sexes are seven inches long and stout billed. In flight, look for short blue wings and tail.

VOICE: The call is a musical *chur-wi* or *tru-ly*. The song is a series of three or four soft musical notes, often described as a warble.

FEEDING: Keen-eyed Eastern Bluebirds feed on ground-dwelling insects, including beetles, crickets, grasshoppers, and caterpillars, which they can spot while perched as far as 150 feet away. They pounce upon their insect prey, then fly to a perch and strike it against a hard surface before feeding—or they just catch and eat insects in the air. Adults also feed juicy, high-protein spiders to nestlings. Wild berries are also eaten, especially in colder months. At feeders, offer raisins, currants, suet mixes, and mealworms (live or freeze-dried).

A young Eastern Bluebird tests its wings. *David Kinneer*

Eastern Bluebird hatchlings already begging for food. *David Kinneer*

Western Bluebird

Sialia mexicana

A male (left) and a female (right) Western Bluebird. *Ashok Khosla*

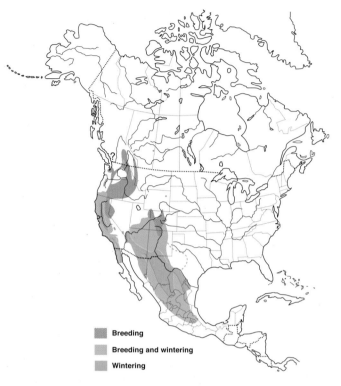

Breeding

Breeding and wintering

Wintering

Western Bluebird populations have declined, although they were once common in the Pacific Northwest's Cascade Range and the Sacramento Valley. A five-year reintroduction project successfully re-established a breeding population on San Juan Island, Washington. Mainland bluebirds were translocated to the islands and provided with nest boxes. Similar reintroduction efforts are ongoing on Canada's Vancouver Island.

RANGE: Western Bluebirds are found in southwestern Canada, Mexico, and many western U.S. states. They are medium- to short-distance migrants that winter in the southern part of their range and begin nesting in early April.

FIELD MARKS: Adult males have cobalt blue wings and tails as well as an all-blue head, chin, and throat, and a white belly. The upper breast is chestnut with varying patterns of blue and gray. The back may be partly or entirely chestnut. Females are a paler, grayer version of the male.

A female Western Bluebird keeps its hatchlings warm in a human-provided nest box. *Steve Simmons*

VOICE: The song is a series of call notes described as *few* or *kew*. Chatter calls sound like *cut-cut-cut*. Soft *tch-tch-tch* calls can also be heard.

FEEDING: Western Bluebirds eat insects in warm weather, and fruits and berries in winter. Mistletoe and juniper berries are favorites, and they love mealworms at feeders. They are often seen "fly catching" or foraging on the ground, using low branches as a jumping-off place.

Mountain Bluebird

Sialia currucoides

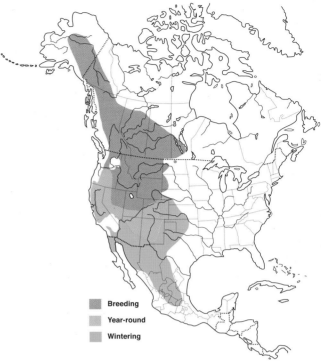

Above: A female (left) and male (right) Mountain Bluebird. The female is carrying nesting material, a sign that this pair is beginning to make a nest. *Russ Amy*

Right: Mountain Bluebirds often arrive so early on their breeding grounds that they are caught in spring snowstorms. This male, looking none too pleased, is huddled to keep warm. *Jim Potter*

Breeding

Year-round

Wintering

Like their Eastern Bluebird cousins, Mountain Bluebirds have difficulty outcompeting nonnative species that reside near farms and ranches year-round. By springtime the non-natives may already have claimed nesting sites. As their name suggests, Mountain Bluebirds will nest at high elevations but are more common at lower elevations.

RANGE: Mountain Bluebirds are found primarily in the western mountains from east-central Alaska to south-central Mexico, migrating to the northern parts of their range to begin nesting in late April.

FIELD MARKS: Breeding males have a turquoise-blue back, a paler blue breast, and white belly and under tail coverts. Females and juveniles are gray above and have pale blue wings and tail and a buffy chest. The adults are slightly larger and thinner-billed than other bluebirds; their wings are proportionately longer than the other bluebird species.

VOICE: The Mountain Bluebird's call is a low *few* or *chur*, described as a soft burry chortle. The male's short, subdued warbling song has been called "hauntingly beautiful."

FEEDING: Mountain Bluebirds feed on insects, including weevils, wasps, beetles, bees, grasshoppers, caterpillars, and crickets. They often "hover hunt" like kestrels when forag-ing, or hunt from low perches before dropping or darting upward to capture prey. In late winter, they rely on native berries of mistletoe, hackberries, juniper, and hollies.

A female Mountain Bluebird keeps her hatchlings warm at Ellis Bird Farm in Alberta, Canada. She will continue to brood them for the next few days. Mountain Bluebirds may lay fewer clutches per breeding season, but their clutches include more eggs than those of either Eastern or Western Bluebirds. *Myrna Pearman*

THE NEST SITE

In southern states, bluebirds may start looking for nesting sites as early as January, so have nest boxes ready for them. However, this may be two to three months later at their northern limit. During the breeding season, check nests at least once a week. Since bluebirds typically lay eggs in the morning, the ideal time to check nests is in the afternoon.

Include perches in your bluebird landscape. Both adult and newly fledged bluebirds like to sit on small trees or fence posts from which they can scout for insects on the ground. Bluebirds are mostly insectivorous, but they also eat wild berries. Offering mealworms near nesting sites, and planting berry-producing grapes, blackberries, dogwood, elderberries, and serviceberries, might induce bluebirds to stay around your property. Supply fresh water for both drinking and bathing.

Many "bluebirders" remove old nesting material from a nest box right after the young have fledged; this task can

A typical clutch of Eastern Bluebird eggs. The nest's inner lining on top is more tightly woven than the outer base. *Bet Zimmerman, sialis.org*

be repeated several times during the nesting season. At the end of the nesting season, clean out the nest box one last time and make any needed repairs. Bluebirds and other species often use nest boxes for roosting in cold weather.

NESTING: Female bluebirds build tight cup nests atop a looser built base. Thin bark strips, pine needles, and dry grasses are typical nesting materials. The inner nest cup may be lined with softer, finer materials.

- EGGS: Range from two to seven pale blue and, very seldom, white eggs. First clutches average five to six eggs; second clutches average four to five eggs. Eastern Bluebirds typically have two clutches a year, but in warmer climates, three clutches are common. In the northern part of their range, Mountain Bluebirds are known to lay larger but fewer clutches than Eastern or Western Bluebirds.
- EGG-LAYING: Typically one egg each day until the clutch is complete.
- INCUBATION: Female incubates for twelve to fifteen days. Male feeds incubating and brooding female.
- FLEDGING: Fledge dates for Eastern and Western Bluebirds may vary from sixteen to nineteen days. Mountain Bluebirds typically fledge within seventeen to twenty-one days.
- POST-FLEDGING: Within a protected wooded area, both bluebird parents feed the fledglings after they leave the nest and while the young are practicing their flying skills. This period may last up to a few weeks after the young learn to fly. The male may continue to assist fledglings while the female begins building a second nest a week or so after the first brood has fledged. First-brood young sometimes help feed their second-brood siblings.

BEHIND THE DESIGN

In the 1960s, self-taught naturalist Dick Peterson noticed the decline of local bluebirds. As a way to help them, he designed a wooden bluebird box to replace their preferred but scarce natural tree holes. His unique "Peterson" nest box, with its signature sloping roof to thwart predators, is credited with helping restore bluebird populations in Minnesota and elsewhere. In the late 1970s, Peterson received an outpouring of letters and requests for nest box plans following a widely read *Minneapolis Star Tribune* article on his bluebird work. Inspired by this surge of

interest, in 1979 Peterson partnered with the National Audubon Society's Minneapolis chapter and formed the Bluebird Recovery Program (BBRP) of Minnesota— the nation's first state bluebird organization. Keith Radel, a BBRP coordinator who knew Peterson, says his legacy extends beyond designing a nest box and founding the organization: "Dick's real influence was teaching people responsible ways to keep birds safe—how to identify and then fix problems at the nest box. His insistence on weekly nest checks has been critical to bluebird recovery."

BEHIND THE DESIGN: THE X-MEN AND THEIR XBOX

In 2010, Dan Sparks, a board member of the North American Bluebird Society (NABS) saw the need for a new kind of bluebird nest box, especially designed for those monitoring multiple nest boxes along "bluebird trails." He, along with many other veteran bluebirders, believed that most common traditional nest boxes could be improved. Some had roofs that tended to warp and leak, others were difficult to open for weekly nest checks; still others were complicated for inexperienced woodworkers to build. Sparks gathered together bluebirders with extensive collective knowledge of nest box design and construction: Kevin Berner, Tom Comfort, Steve Eno, Steve Gilbertson, Keith Kridler, and Keith Radel.

NABS board member Tom Comfort recalls, "The committee was enthusiastic, and what could have been a long and laborious process actually moved swiftly. Even though regional differences of weather and predators meant that one nest box couldn't fit all needs, most agreed on the basic requirements of a simple new nest box."

A plan emerged: To come up with nest box that was attractive to bluebirds, simple in design and construction, easy to monitor, and resistant to inclement weather and predators. "Nest boxes are often named for their designers or creators," observed Comfort. So how to name this nest box, designed by a committee? Box "X" became the Xbox, a simple, inexpensive, easy-to-build front-opening nest box with an inner roof that provides a second level of protection.

Southern bluebirder Fred Stille—engineer by trade, woodworker by obsession—was pleased to put his skills to work by drawing up the X-Mens' woodworking plans. "My motive is to help the birds, by helping people help the birds," Stille says.

The committee seems to have met its goal. So far, the Xbox is reportedly providing a dry, safe nesting environment in a variety of different regions. "I believe that the Xbox is making history," Comfort says.

PLACING THE NEST BOX: Eastern Bluebirds prefer forest clearings and semi-open country with scattered trees. Big yards, orchards, and cemeteries are good nest box sites. The preferred nesting habitats for Mountain Bluebirds consist of short grass areas interspersed by a few trees. Western Bluebirds can be found in woodland edges and open, park-like forests, including those that have been thinned or lightly logged. Space individual or paired bluebird nest boxes at least 300 feet apart or out of the line of sight from the nearest bluebird nest box.

- MOUNTING: The Xbox is designed to be mounted onto a half-inch conduit/rebar pole, called the "Gilbertson system" (described in more detail in Chapter 2). Avoid mounting nest boxes on fences or trees where climbing mammals or snakes are present. Use predator guards to further block nest box access.
- HEIGHT: Bluebirds nest within a wide range of heights, from two to fifty feet. Mounting at eye level provides easy checking; however, if cats or other predators are problems, hang nest boxes at least six to eight feet from the ground.

Western Bluebird chicks huddle together inside the nest box.
Steve Simmons

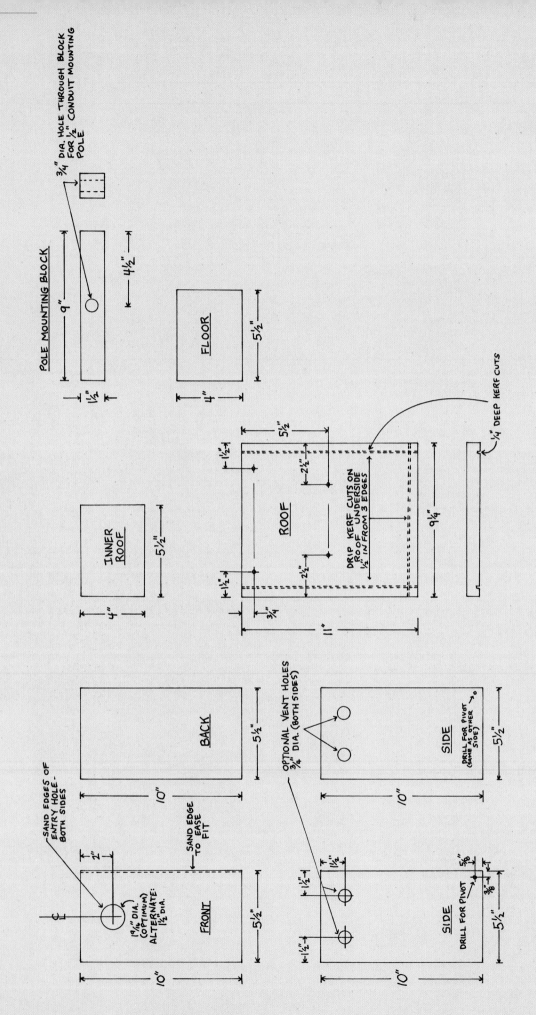

XBOX BLUEBIRD NEST BOX
DESIGN BY: DAN SPARKS AND THE X-MEN
DRAWN BY: CHRIS WILLETT
(NOT TO SCALE)

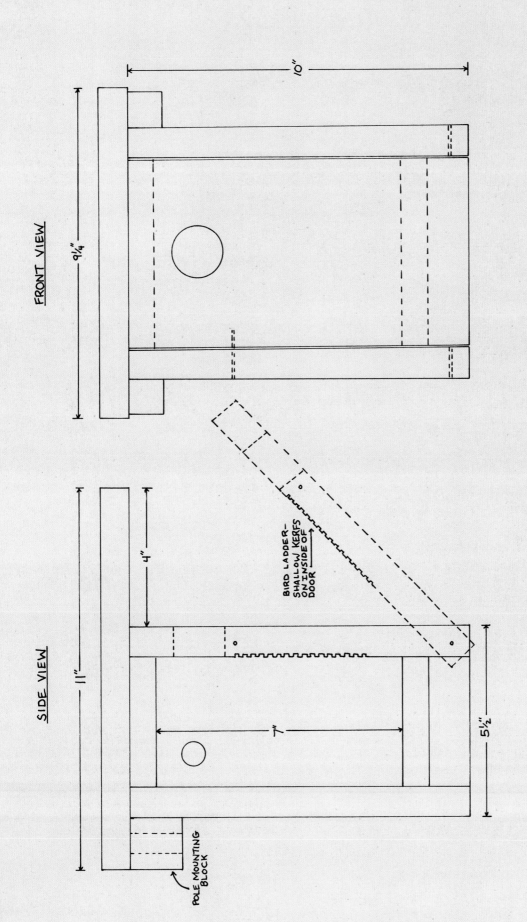

FRONT VIEW

10"

9¼"

SIDE VIEW

11"

4"

7"

5½"

BIRD LADDER—
SHALLOW KERFS
ON INSIDE OF
DOOR

POLE MOUNTING
BLOCK

XBOX BLUEBIRD NEST BOX
DESIGN BY: DAN SPARKS AND THE X-MEN
DRAWN BY: CHRIS WILLETT
(NOT TO SCALE)

XBOX BLUEBIRD NEST BOX

DESIGNED BY DAN SPARKS AND THE X-MEN

MATERIALS

- Lumber: cypress (used here), white cedar, hemlock, or local weather-resistant wood with low toxicity

- One 1x10x11" (roof)

- Four 1x6x10" (front, sides, and back)

- Two 1x6x4" (floor and inner roof)

- One 2x2x9" (pole-mounting block)

- Exterior screws: twelve 1⅝" (basic construction); two to six 1¼" (roof to inner roof); and two 2" (pole mounting block to back)

- Caulk or sealant (sealing between top and inner roof)

- One 2½" galvanized nail (bent, latch nail)

- Mounting: One ½"x5' galvanized metal conduit, one ½"x4'–5' steel rebar (for stake), and one conduit coupler (see Gilbertson sidebar, page 22)

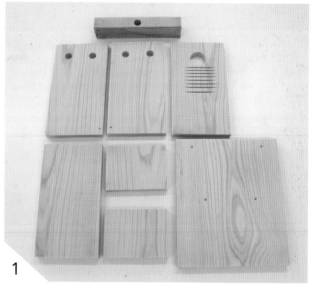

1

Hole saws were used for the Xbox entrance and ventilation holes, as well as the mounting block. A table saw with its blade lowered was used for the drip kerfs on the underside of the roof and for the ladder kerfs on the inside of the front.

2

The back piece of the Xbox is attached to the inner roof. Two deck screws (1⅝") are installed with an impact driver.

3

Test-fit the attached back, unattached sides and inner roof. Use a pencil to mark the placement of the recessed floor. Drive in screws.

4

Top of sides are attached to the inner roof above the entry hole.

5

Pivot screws, driven into the front piece from the bottom of both sides, allow the front to open easily for checking and cleaning.

6

One galvanized nail (2½") is bent to create the latch nail. Drill the latch nail hole slightly downward.

7

The mounting block for the Gilbertson pole system is installed on the back of the Xbox with two exterior deck screws (2"). Note the predrilled ¾" hole on the mounting block.

8

Apply a bead (line) of all-purpose low VOC caulk to the top of the inner roof prior to installing the exterior roof.

9

The Gilbertson pole system is easy to assemble. Drive rebar into the ground, leaving two feet above ground. Attach conduit coupler to end of conduit. Tighten upper, shorter screw against conduit. Slip coupler over rebar. Tighten lower, longer screw against rebar. Clean pole with steel wool and coat it with furniture polish. Add baffle if needed.

The Xbox is placed onto the Gilbertson conduit/rebar pole, ready to become home for bluebirds and others.

FLYCATCHERS

Ash-throated Flycatcher

Myiarchus cinerascens

Breeding

Breeding and winter

Winter

An Ash-throated Flycatcher in Palo Alto, California. *Ashok Khosla*

Great Crested Flycatcher

Myiarchus crinitus

Breeding

Year-round

Wintering

A Great Crested Flycatcher catches the sun in Great Falls, Virginia.
Ruhikanta Meetei

Some Southern California Ash-throated Flycatcher populations have been greatly reduced by habitat loss. Conversely, Great Crested Flycatchers have benefited from deciduous forest fragmentation, which has increased the woodland edges where they hunt for insects. Logging and development have made nesting cavities scarce for both species.

RANGE: Ash-throated Flycatchers reside throughout the Southwest, California, and as far north as central Washington, Idaho, Wyoming, and south into Mexico. They overwinter in Mexico and Central America. Great Crested Flycatchers are summer residents throughout southern Canada and the eastern United States. Most winter from Mexico to South America.

FIELD MARKS: Great Crested Flycatcher adults are almost 9 inches long, with a 13-inch wingspan, bright yellow belly and under tail, olive-gray underparts, cinnamon-rufous wings and tail, pale wing bars, and a prominent raised crest. Ash-throated Flycatchers are slightly smaller, paler versions of the Great Crested.

VOICE: Great Crested Flycatchers are easier to hear than to see. Their distinctive "police whistle" call is a strong, rising *wee-eep* or *queEEEEP!* Ash-throated Flycatchers have a short, abrupt *bik* or *kaBRIK* call.

FEEDING: Flycatchers hunt primarily in the tree canopy for large insects and small fruits. They glean insects from leaves and tree bark, drop down to capture insects on the ground, or fly from perch to perch to catch airborne flying insects, a maneuver called "sallying."

A varied collection of materials within a Wood Duck nest box cushions these purple-streaked Great Crested Flycatcher eggs. A parasitic Brown-headed Cowbird laid the middle egg. *Aaron Ward, courtesy of the Maryland Wood Duck Initiative*

THE NEST SITE

Protecting forest edges, preserving tall trees and dead snags, and installing nest boxes all enhance flycatcher territory and potential nest sites. Researcher Michael Morrison notes a marked preference for hanging or swinging boxes, which are less subject to predation or starling invasion than stationary boxes.

NESTING: Where natural tree cavities are limited, flycatchers take to nest boxes—along with mailboxes, rain gutters, and other inventive places. Nests contain dry grasses, leaves, hair, fur, feathers, rootlets, string, small twigs, bark, paper, crinkly materials such as plastic wrappers, and occasionally, especially in Great Crested Flycatcher nests, shed snakeskins. Rabbit fur often lines Ash-throated Flycatcher nests.
- EGGS: Four to eight creamy white to pinkish eggs with brownish or purplish streaks and blotches. Ash-throated eggs are less streaked.
- EGG-LAYING: One per day.
- INCUBATION: Thirteen to fifteen days. Female incubates; both parents feed chicks.
- DAYS TO FLEDGE: Thirteen to fifteen days.

PLACING THE NEST BOX: These two species prefer different habitats: arid brush country for Ash-throated Flycatchers and open deciduous woodlands for the Great Crested.
- NESTING MATERIALS: Add small amounts (one to two inches) of wood chips to the nest box.
- MOUNTING: Mount onto a half-inch conduit/rebar pole, called the "Gilbertson system." Avoid mounting nest boxes on fences or trees where climbing mammals or snakes are present. Use predator guards to further block nest box access.
- HEIGHT: Mounting at eye level provides easy checking; however, if cats or other predators are problems, hang nest boxes at least six to eight feet from the ground.

THE BUILD

Flycatchers will nest in an Xbox: see pages 52–53 for the plan. Ideal entry hole sizes are one and one-half inches for Ash-throated Flycatcher and one and three-quarters inches for Great Crested Flycatcher.

SWALLOWS

Tree Swallow

Tachycineta bicolor

The young female Tree Swallow (left) is less colorful than the male (right). With age, female Tree Swallows become less drab and brown and more closely resemble males. *David Kinneer*

Summer / Breeding
Nonbreeding

Violet-green Swallow

Tachycineta thalassina

Violet-green Swallows are aerial feeders, subsisting primarily on a diet of flying insects. *Ashok Khosla*

Breeding
Year-round
Nonbreeding

Tree Swallows are common and widespread, but their populations have declined recently, which may be due to loss or degradation of nesting habitat. Violet-green Swallow populations are stable. Both species are readily attracted to bluebird nest boxes, though some people recommend roomier houses.

RANGE: Unlike other swallows that winter in South America, Tree Swallows migrate to the southern United States and Mexico. This shorter migration enables an earlier return to the northeast—an advantage in claiming nest sites. Violet-green Swallows breed in western North America from central Alaska and western Canada, south to Mexico.

FIELD MARKS: Tree Swallows are steely blue or green above with glistening white underparts. They are about five and a half inches long with a fourteen and a half-inch wingspan; wingtips reach the tail tip. In flight, this small, broad-winged bird has a white underside and forked tail and glides in circles. Three or four quick flaps are often followed by a short climb. Violet-green Swallows have emerald-green backs and white above the eye. Wings are narrower; tails are shorter. In both species, females are duller and browner.

VOICE: The call is a liquid twittering *cheet* or *chi-veet*. Song resembles *weet, trit, weet*, with variations.

FEEDING: Both Tree Swallows and Violet-green Swallows feed on flying ants, beetles, flies, and occasionally, bees, wasps, and grasshoppers. These adaptable birds also land on beaches to pick tiny insects and crustaceans from the sand. In cold weather, when insects are scarce, they switch to fruits like bayberry, or seeds from bulrush, sedge, and smartweed.

THE NEST SITE

In early spring, mount pairs of clean, bluebird-sized nest boxes about twenty feet apart, to provide for a pair of both swallows and bluebirds. Research shows that swallow nests with an ample feather lining have better chick survival than those without. Provide chicken feathers in a hanging basket or toss feathers to the wind and let the swallows snatch them from the air.

NESTING: Originally woodpecker cavity nesters, swallows readily use nest boxes. Females build their nests using fine grasses with a feather lining that insulates eggs in chilly early spring weather. Males may have two mates simultaneously.

- EGGS: Four to six white eggs.
- EGG-LAYING: One per day.
- INCUBATION: Thirteen days. Female incubates; both parents feed young.
- DAYS TO FLEDGE: About twenty days.

PLACING THE NEST BOX: Cluster nest boxes in the center of a large open field. Rural areas near "buggy" wetlands are a plus. Placing nest boxes far from buildings, woods, or hedgerows allows swallows to spot incoming predators at a distance and use their flying ability to escape.

- MOUNTING: Mount onto a half-inch conduit/rebar pole, called the "Gilbertson system." Avoid mounting nest boxes on fences or trees where climbing mammals or snakes are present. Use predator guards to further block nest box access.
- HEIGHT: Mounting at eye level provides easy checking; however, if cats or other predators are problems, hang nest boxes at least six to eight feet from the ground.

THE BUILD

Tree Swallows and Violet-green Swallows will nest in an Xbox: See page 52–53 for plans. Nestlings rely on the kerf ladder of the Xbox—if there's no ladder, they can get trapped inside. Ideal entry hole size is one and one-half inches.

TITMICE

Tufted Titmouse

Baeolophus bicolor

Year-round

Note the characteristic black feathers just above this Tufted Titmouse's bill. *David Kinneer*

Titmice are common, grayish, small-crested birds whose populations seem to be thriving. They are year-round residents. Over the last half-century, Tufted Titmice have expanded their range farther north, perhaps due to warming climates, the reversion of farmlands to forests, and increased bird feeding.

RANGE: Tufted Titmice are common in most eastern states in deciduous forests below 2,000 feet in elevation. The Black-crested Titmouse of Texas and northeastern Mexico has recently been given separate species status. These two species overlap in central Texas. The Oak Titmouse is found from southern Oregon to Baja California. The Juniper Titmouse inhabits the Great Basin region, west of Texas, and as far north as southeastern Oregon.

FIELD MARKS: At six inches long, with a ten-inch wingspan, the Tufted Titmouse is all gray above, whitish below, with pale rust-colored flanks, a tufted crest, large black eyes, and a small square of black feathers on the forehead just above the black bill. Juveniles have a pale face and lack the dark facial feathers. Black-crested Titmice are similar to the Tufted, except for the darker crest. Oak and Juniper Titmice are nearly identical. They are smaller and duller brown than the Tufted and Black-crested Titmice.

VOICE: Tufted Titmice calls are wheezy and nasal, similar to chickadees. The song is a low, loud, clear whistle: *peter, peter, peter,* or *here, here, here!* Black-crested sounds like Tufted but may sing a higher pitch and at a faster pace. Oak Titmice repeat strong whistled phrases. Juniper Titmice sing lower-pitched songs that lack the pure whistle quality.

FEEDING: Frequent feeder visitors, these birds favor acorns, beechnuts, and caterpillars in the wild. They also eat a variety of insects and fruit, especially blackberries, blueberries, elderberries, junipers, mulberries, wild cherries, sumac, poison ivy, and bayberries.

Oak Titmouse
Baeolophus inornatus

Juniper Titmouse
Baeolophus ridgwayi

The Oak Titmouse is gray-brown all over. *Ashok Khosla*

A Juniper Titmouse sings in its namesake tree. *Ashok Khosla*

Oak Titmouse
Juniper Titmouse

THE NEST SITE

Set out nest boxes to attract titmice in early spring. As a further enticement, offer nesting materials like dog and cat fur. Plant berry bushes at the forest edge; provide peanuts, sunflower seeds, and suet at the feeders. Clean out nest boxes after the nesting season. Keep them up all winter for roosting titmice.

NESTING: At nesting time, males court females with gifts of food; her high-pitched calls are accompanied by begging behavior. Females build the nest, although males help gather materials. Nests are made with mostly moss, leaves, and bark and are lined with a variety of softer materials, including feathers, fur, wool, and hair.

- EGGS: Usually five to seven, but they can range from four to nine creamy, brown-speckled eggs.
- EGG-LAYING: One per day.
- INCUBATION: Thirteen to fourteen days for Tufted and Black-crested; fourteen to sixteen days for Oak and Juniper Titmice. Female incubates.
- DAYS TO FLEDGE: Fifteen to eighteen days for Tufted and Black-crested; a few days longer for the western titmice. May be cared for by parents three to four weeks past fledging.

Black-crested Titmouse

Baeolophus atricristatus

The Black-crested Titmouse is found in Texas, Oklahoma, and east-central Mexico. *Ashok Khosla*

PLACING THE NEST BOX: Place the nest box in a forested area. Tufted Titmice have adapted to urban areas, too, particularly those with large oak and beech trees.

- MOUNTING: Mount onto a half-inch conduit/rebar pole, called the "Gilbertson system." Avoid mounting nest boxes on fences or trees where climbing mammals or snakes are present. Use predator guards to further block nest box access.
- HEIGHT: Mounting at eye level provides easy checking; however, if cats or other predators are problems, hang nest boxes at least six to eight feet from the ground.

THE BUILD

These species of titmice will nest in an Xbox: see pages 52–53 for plans. Ideal entry hole size is one and one-quarter inches.

QUICK TIP

Specific-sized entry holes, as well as optional "entry hole reducers" or "restrictors" can protect small birds (like titmice and chickadees) that are already using a bluebird nest box. Smaller entry holes obstruct larger birds like starlings and bluebirds, which will aggressively compete for nest boxes.

Barred Owl   *Strix varia*

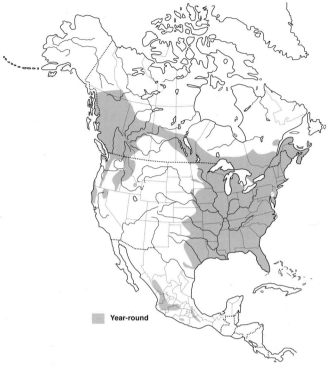

Year-round

This Barred Owl is well camouflaged within the old-growth cypress-tupelo swamplands of Audubon's Francis Beidler Forest in South Carolina.
Mark Musselman

Barred Owls originally resided mostly in mature, moist, undisturbed forests in eastern North America; they have since suffered from deforestation that removed large nesting trees. During the past century, these birds have spread north and west. They now reside in coniferous Pacific Northwest forests, where they compete with the threatened Spotted Owl. Barred Owls are preyed upon by Great Horned Owls, and those that nest in suburbia are at risk from car collisions.

RANGE: These nonmigratory owls are widely distributed throughout the United States and Canada.

FIELD MARKS: Barred Owls average eighteen and a half inches long with forty-inch wingspans. Large and stocky, these mottled gray-brown and white owls have rounded heads, large dark brown eyes, and orange-yellow bills. Brown vertical stripes or "bars" on the belly give the bird its common name.

VOICE: The Barred Owl has a distinctive eight- or nine-note hooting call, often described as "Who cooks for you? Who cooks for you-all?" Courtship calling between males and females can turn into loud, cackling duets.

FEEDING: Barred Owls are nocturnal "sit-and-wait" predators, looking and listening from an elevated perch, then flying silently to capture prey. Their varied diet includes mice, voles, squirrels, chipmunks, small birds, and young rabbits, as well as fish, amphibians, reptiles, and invertebrates.

THE NEST SITE

Eggs may be laid in January in the deep South, but typically later in northern regions. Practices that benefit Barred Owls include allowing some trees to reach maturity, retaining nesting snags, and providing nest boxes.

NESTING: Barred Owls are monogamous and prefer large, unfragmented forests, which support a higher diversity of prey; larger, taller trees are also more likely to have natural cavities for nesting. Nest sites are usually near water, in deciduous trees, broken snags, or human-made nest boxes.

- EGGS: Two to five, with an average of three white eggs; single brood.
- EGG-LAYING: One to three days between first and second egg; two to four between second and third.
- INCUBATION: Twenty-eight to thirty-three days; female incubates.

- DAYS TO FLEDGE: Four to five weeks; parents continue to feed fledglings.

PLACING THE NEST BOX: Attach securely to a large, deciduous tree in a mature forest, near water if possible. Prey availability may influence nest-site selection.

- NESTING MATERIALS: Line nest box with several inches of hard wood mulch, pine straw, or leaves.
- MOUNTING: Use caution when mounting these large, heavy boxes. Face box opening sideways for easy access.
- HEIGHT: Fifteen to twenty feet.

Two-week-old Barred Owls—mostly beaks and fluff.
Rob Bierregaard

A Barred Owl roosting in a nest box in Charlotte, North Carolina, in late February. *Brad Kuntz*

BEHIND THE DESIGN

Rob Bierregaard credits the community service program at New York's Millbrook High School for steering him toward a career in ornithology. There, he was put in charge of caring for "Shakespeare," the campus zoo's Barred Owl. Years later, while teaching at the University of North Carolina's Charlotte campus, he established a Barred Owl project to study the locally abundant suburban populations. Over the years, the nest box design he used with students evolved into a "McMansion"— a one-family home with plenty of room for the youngsters and easy access for the adults. The true success of his design is in the data: to date, the project nest boxes have produced fledglings from more than 100 nests. In addition to studying Barred Owls, Bierregaard uses satellite telemetry to research osprey migration and nesting. He is also editor of two books on his research on Amazon rain forest ecology and conservation.

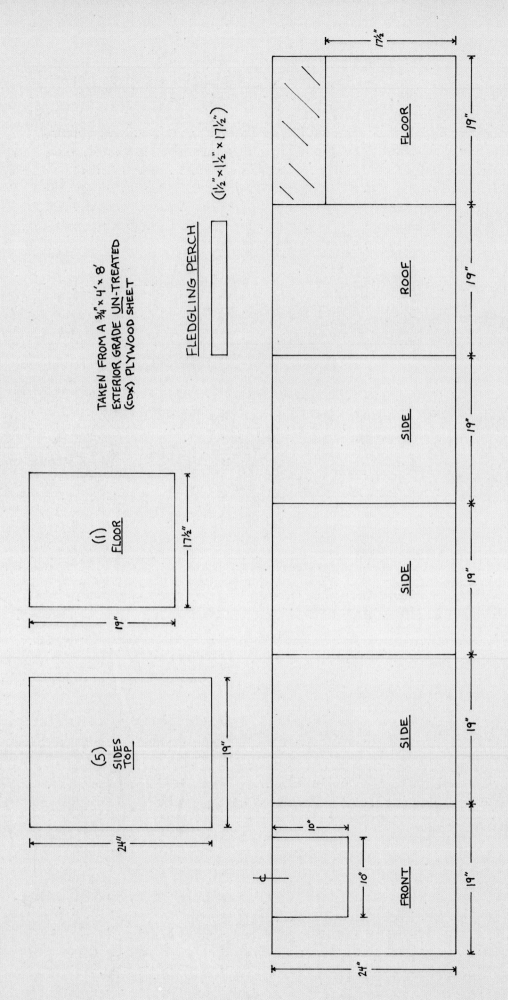

TAKEN FROM A ¾" × 4' × 8'
EXTERIOR GRADE UN-TREATED
(CDX) PLYWOOD SHEET

FLEDGLING PERCH
(1½" × 1½" × 17½")

(1)
FLOOR
17½"
19"

(5)
SIDES
TOP
19"
24"

FLOOR
17½"
19"

ROOF
19"

SIDE
19"

SIDE
19"

SIDE
19"

FRONT
10"
10"
c
24"
19"

BARRED OWL NEST BOX
DESIGN BY: RICHARD O. BIERREGAARD
DRAWN BY: CHRIS WILLETT
(NOT TO SCALE)

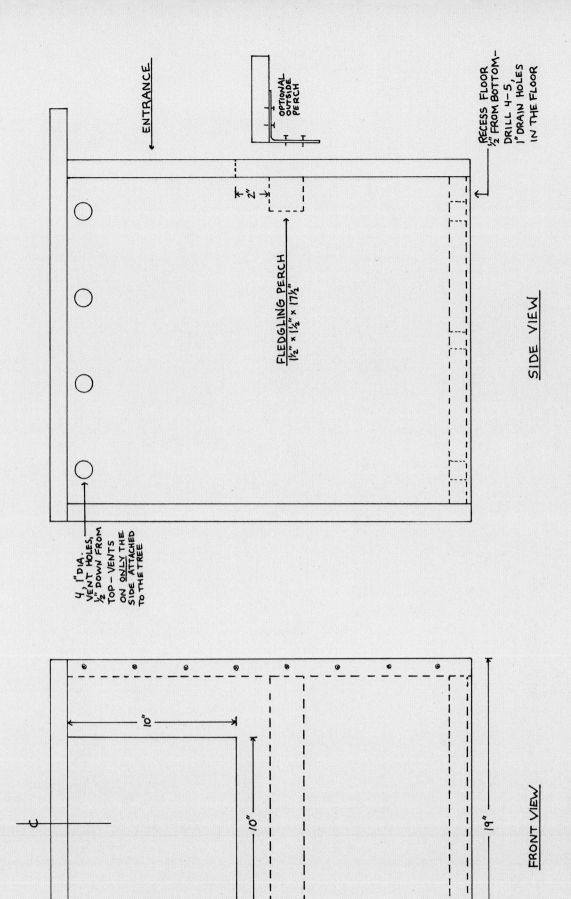

ENTRANCE

OPTIONAL OUTSIDE PERCH

RECESS FLOOR ½" FROM BOTTOM—
DRILL 4–5, 1" DRAIN HOLES IN THE FLOOR

2"

FLEDGLING PERCH
1½" × 1½" × 17½"

SIDE VIEW

4, 1" DIA. VENT HOLES, 1½" DOWN FROM TOP—VENTS ON ONLY THE SIDE ATTACHED TO THE TREE

10"

10"

C

19"

FRONT VIEW

BARRED OWL NEST BOX
DESIGN BY: RICHARD O. BIERREGAARD
DRAWN BY: CHRIS WILLETT
(NOT TO SCALE)

BARRED OWL NEST BOX

DESIGNED BY RICHARD O. BIERREGAARD

1

Cut the pieces out according to the diagrams. You'll have five pieces 24x19". These will be the four sides of the box plus the top. Cut the 19"x17½" floor out of the second sheet of plywood.

MATERIALS

- One sheet of ¾"x4'x8' exterior CDX, untreated plywood. Cut the ¾"x4'x8' exterior CDX sheet in half lengthwise, to create two pieces, each ¾"x 2'x8'

- Roughly thirty 2" exterior-grade deck screws.

- Exterior wood glue

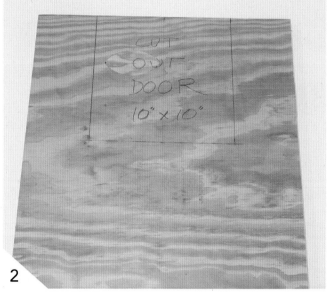

2

Mark the 10"x10" entrance door. Cut with a circular saw, a jigsaw, or a handsaw.

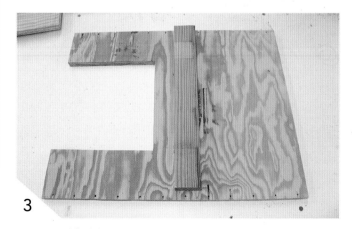

3

An optional fledgling perch (1½"x1½"x17½") can be added to the interior of the box, just below the door. At this stage, all exterior pieces can be stained with a low VOC wood preservative. The roof of a plywood box wears better with a finish.

QUICK TIPS

Hanging this heavy nest box can be tricky. It's a good idea to do this job with several people. One way is to secure a long rope around the box. Tie a weight on the end of the loose rope and throw it over a branch, just above where you want to put the box. Pull up box to desired site. Designer Rob Bierregaard advises using a rope and pulley system to get the box up into the tree.

Unlike most tree-hung nest boxes, the entry door of the Barred Owl nest box faces sideways, with one of the sides of the nest box—not the back—resting on the tree. Position the nest box accordingly. This way, a ladder can be steadied against the tree, not the nest box, a safer method for accessing a nest box fifteen to twenty feet high. Note: Since this nest box does not have a side or top that opens, all necessary access—to remove squirrel nests in fall, for example—is through the large entry door.

Once the box is in place, hang it securely. A preferred method passes a ³⁄₁₆" to ¼" diameter vinyl-coated wire rope through two predrilled upper corner ⅜" holes on the side that leans against the tree trunk. Loop wire rope over a strong branch or pre-positioned, half-driven ⅜" diameter, 6" long lag screw on opposite side of the tree trunk. Clamp the ends of the wire rope together around the tree.

4

Test-fit sides. Then predrill all screw locations. Just before assembling, glue all edges that will attach to each other. Gluing edges adds strength and water tightness.

5

Don't spare the screws, especially around the sides. Place them every four to six inches. Make sure no screws protrude into the box, where they might injure the birds.

6

Recess the floor ½" . Drill four or five 1" diameter drainage holes into the floor.

7

Note the roof overhang, an important feature for all nest boxes.

8

If you're going to use hexhead lag screws to mount the box to the tree, drill four or five holes near the middle of the side (not the back) of the box you will attach to the tree. The holes should be the size of your lag screws. Use a washer between the box and lag screw, and don't tighten them hard against the tree. As the tree grows, it can push a box right off the screws. Leave ¼" or ½" of play in a couple of the lag screws to account for the tree's growth. If you're going to use wire cable to hang the box, drill two to four holes at the top of the side of the box that will be against the tree. Pass the cable through the holes and clamp the ends of the wire together around the tree.

Option: Stain all the exterior sides with a deck preservative before assembly.

Drill four vent holes (1"diameter) on the side of the Barred Owl nest box that will not be against the tree, and mount it appropriately.

OWLS

Eastern Screech-Owl   *Otus asio*

Year-round

Gray phase of the Eastern Screech-Owl, looking a little bit sleepy.
Mark Mussleman

Western Screech-Owl   *Otus kennicottii*

Year-round

This Western Screech-Owl's plumage keeps it well-camouflaged
amidst tree bark. *Ashok Khosla*

Four Eastern Screech-Owl fledglings out on a limb in central Texas. They range in age from twenty-five to twenty-eight days old.
Chris W. Johnson

Their small size, excellent camouflage, unfussy nesting habits, and varied diet make Eastern and Western Screech-Owls successful survivors. The eastern birds adjust well to human presence. In fact, suburbs may provide more prey, milder climates, and fewer predators than rural areas. Western Screech-Owls choose higher, drier habitats. Territories of these two species, formerly classified as one, can overlap. The two species are also known to hybridize. Both Barred Owls and Great Horned Owls prey on the much smaller screech owls.

RANGE: Eastern Screech-Owls reside year round primarily east of the Rocky Mountains. Western Screech-Owls are found in the southwestern, western, and northwestern states up into Alaska.

FIELD MARKS: These diminutive owls are about nine inches tall with twenty-inch wingspans and strongly barred underparts. Females are slightly larger than males. Characteristic ear tufts are lacking in the young. Although Eastern and Western Screech-Owls closely resemble each other, the bills are yellow-greenish in eastern owls and black in western owls. Eastern owls are gray or reddish-brown; western owls are gray or brown.

BEHIND THE DESIGN

Although biologist Fred Gehlbach also studies Western Screech-Owls in Arizona, he knows Eastern Screech-Owls best. Upon moving to central Texas to teach at Baylor University in the early 1960s, he was intrigued by a pair of owls popping out of a fox squirrel box. He has been studying the nesting habits of rural and suburban screech owls and telling their stories ever since. Gehlbach examined the owls' natural tree cavity nests, created three different nest box designs, and tested them all. Outdoor plywood, pine, and cedar all worked well: "The more weathered the better," notes Gehlbach, and an eight-inch-square floor size was "just fine." Gehlbach also found that these owls fare better in suburbia than rural areas. "Life is easier there," he explains. Spacious lawns and open spaces are good places to hunt, and backyard bird feeders offer up small-feathered prey. Gehlbach's book, *Eastern Screech Owl: Life History, Ecology, and Behavior in the Suburbs and Countryside*, is in its second printing (2008).

This red phase Eastern Screech-Owl pair made a Wood Duck nest box their home.
Aaron Ward, courtesy of the Maryland Wood Duck Initiative

VOICE: Eastern birds utter a mournful tremulous, descending trilling call, described as a whinny. Western birds emit a series of short whistles described as a bouncing ball call. Both birds "bark" when alarmed.

FEEDING: Screech owls begin feeding after dusk. These nocturnal generalists eat night-flying insects, small mammals, and birds alike, then regurgitate pellets of feathers, fur, and bones.

THE NEST SITE

Eastern Screech-Owls begin nesting in February in southern states but may wait until July in far northern habitats. Provide birdbaths for drinking and bathing and nest boxes for seasonal nesting, as well as for roosting and storing prey year-round. Western Screech-Owls use nest boxes less readily than their eastern counterparts.

(Data are for the more widely studied Eastern Screech-Owl)
NESTING: Males bring food to females at potential nest sites. Once chosen, the male guards and defends the area surrounding the nest site.
- EGGS: Usually four to five white or cream-colored eggs.
- EGG-LAYING: The first few eggs are often laid two days apart, then one per day.

- INCUBATION: Twenty-six days. Female incubates; both parents feed young.
- DAYS TO FLEDGE: Twenty-eight days after hatching.

PLACING THE NEST BOX: Shaded areas in sparse woods, streamside forests, farmland, suburban backyards, and city parks. Avoid facing the nest box north. Face the entry hole east or south where possible, as the birds like to sit in the entranceway (even during the day) to soak up sunlight.
- NESTING MATERIALS: Add a couple of inches of wood chips or dry leaves.
- MOUNTING: Attach to straight trees wider than the box or install on posts or buildings.
- HEIGHT: About ten feet high.

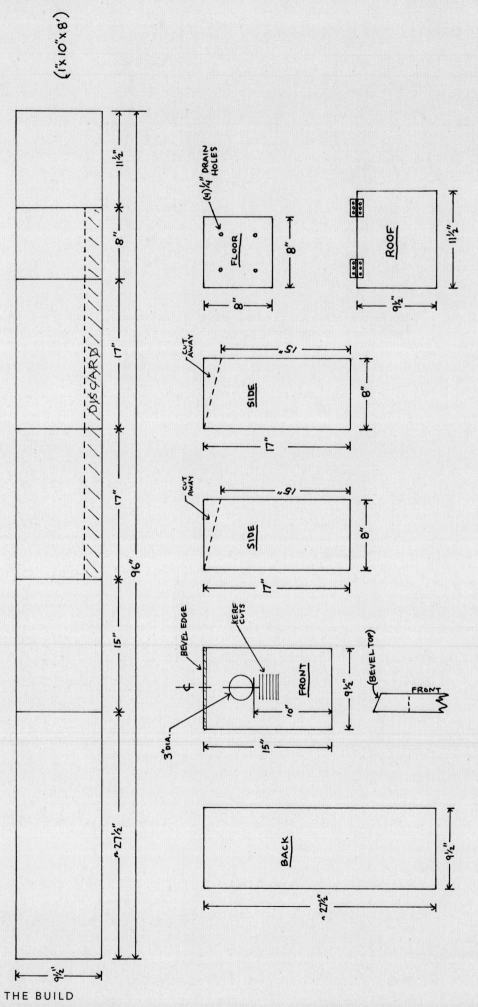

SCREECH-OWL NEST BOX

DESIGN BY: FRED GEHLBACH
DRAWN BY: CHRIS WILLETT
(NOT TO SCALE)

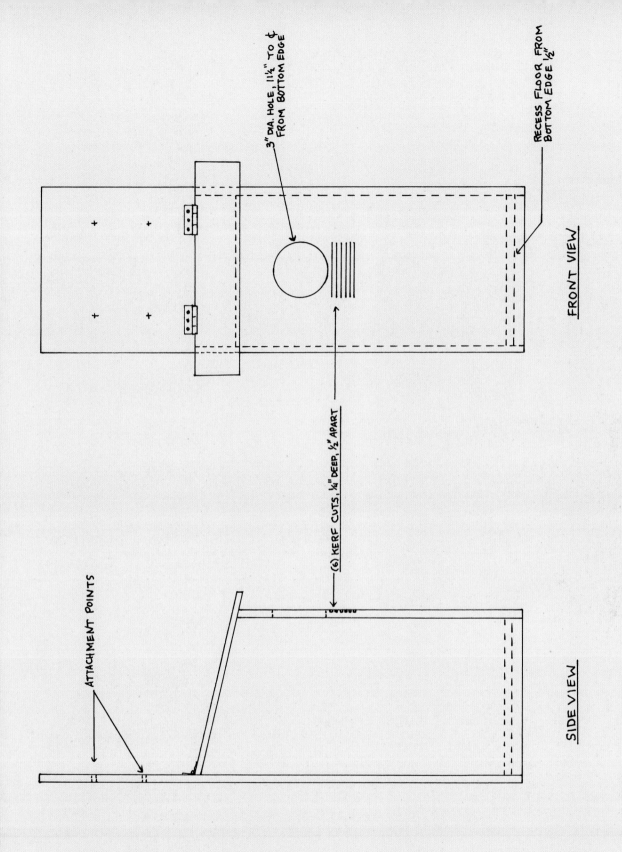

3" DIA. HOLE, 11¼" TO ₵ FROM BOTTOM EDGE

RECESS FLOOR FROM BOTTOM EDGE ½"

FRONT VIEW

(6) KERF CUTS, ¼" DEEP, ½" APART

ATTACHMENT POINTS

SIDE VIEW

SCREECH-OWL NEST BOX
DESIGN BY: FRED GEHLBACH
DRAWN BY: CHRIS WILLETT
(NOT TO SCALE)

SCREECH-OWL NEST BOX

DESIGNED BY FRED GEHLBACH

1

Cut pieces according to the drawing. Measure and cut out the 3" entrance hole on the front piece (be certain you measure up from the bottom 10" to the bottom of the hole). Make four or five kerf cuts on the exterior of the box, the same width as the entrance hole. Cuts are ½" apart and ¼" deep.

MATERIALS

- One 1"x10"x8' cypress (used here) or cedar board (¾" thick)
- Two 1½x1½" exterior hinges with hinge screws
- Approximately thirty 2" exterior-grade deck screws

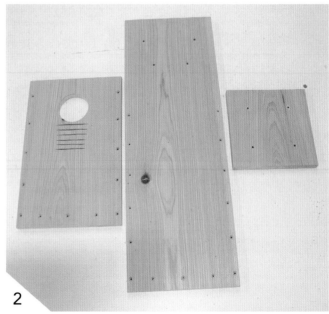

2

Drill out ¼" drain holes on the floor piece. Start assembly of pieces by laying out the back piece and placing the sides on it. Mark and predrill pieces accordingly. Attach sides to the back piece. Predrill the floor piece and screw to sides.

3

Be certain to recess the floor piece ½″ from the bottom, to prevent water seepage into the nest cavity.

4

Attach the predrilled front piece to the sides and floor. Be sure that the front piece is aligned with the angle of the sides, as this allows for a tight fit of the roof.

5

Place the roof piece on top of the sides and make sure it's centered.

6

Attach the hinges to the roof so that they are equal distance apart (approximately 1½″ in from the edge of the roof). Attach the hinge to the back piece. Drill mounting holes in the back piece.

7

The Screech-Owl nest box is ready to hang onto a tree or post or building. Opposite page: The nest box was attached to a tall, straight pine with two ¼″ diameter, 4″ long galvanized lag screws driven into the back piece, with a washer between screws and board.

FLICKERS

Northern Flicker

Colaptes auratus

Male red-shafted Northern Flickers sport a red "mustache."
Ashok Khosla

Breeding
Year-round
Wintering

A female yellow-shafted Northern Flicker. Flickers spend much of their time on the ground looking for ants, this species' favorite meal. *Ashok Khosla*

Flicker populations have been declining since the late 1960s, which is a matter of concern, as these ant-loving woodpeckers play an important role in woodland communities. In the soft wood of dead or dying trees, they excavate cavities that are later used by other birds. Competition with House Sparrows and starlings for nest cavities, and the development of fields and open land, have made this once-abundant bird less common.

RANGE: Northern Flickers occur in sparsely wooded regions across North America. Birds that breed far north migrate south and east.

FIELD MARKS: Brownish overall, this thirteen-inch long bird has a twenty-inch wingspan, a gray-brown crown, black chest patch, and spotted beige breast. Once considered two species, "yellow-shafted" Northern Flickers east of the Rockies show yellow underwings; "red-shafted" flickers, west of the Rockies, show red. Adult males have a red (east) or black mustache (west). All show conspicuous white rumps in flight.

VOICE: Call is a loud, descending *klee-yer*, and a rapid, squeaky *flick-a, flick-a, flick-a*. A soft *wik-a-wik-a-wik-a* is made by nesting adults. Males drum on trees or other objects—including houses—to defend their territory.

A male yellow-shafted Northern Flicker feeds a youngster at a Michigan nest box. Males can be identified by a black "mustache." Long cuts on the outer nest box surface help flickers keep a firm hold. *Allen Bower*

This flicker nest box contains nine glossy white eggs—a high number for this woodpecker. Notice the kerfs all around the inside of the nest box. *Allen Bower*

FEEDING: Flickers are often on the ground, hammering ant hills and lapping up ants and ant eggs with their long, sticky tongues. Wood-boring beetles, beetle larvae, wasps, grasshoppers, crickets, berries, and other fruits are on the menu, too.

THE NEST SITE

Flickers adapt well to living near humans and are more likely to use nest boxes than other woodpeckers. Hang flicker nest boxes by February. Pack the entire nest box, especially the entry hole, with softwood chips to discourage sparrows and starlings, and encourage flickers to "excavate" a cavity, just as they would naturally. If flickers abandon a nest box taken over by starlings, refill the nest box with wood chips. Birds may use nest boxes as winter roosts, too. Leave dead and dying trees standing for natural cavity nest sites. Plant elderberry, serviceberry, and dogwood trees. Suet and hulled sunflower seeds may entice flickers to feeders.

NESTING: Both sexes excavate tree cavities or nest boxes filled with soft wood chips. The nest consists of a bed of wood chips.

- EGGS: Usually five to eight glossy white eggs. High numbers of eggs could be the result of nonrelated females "dumping" eggs into another female's nest.
- EGG-LAYING: One per day.
- INCUBATION: Eleven to fourteen days. Both parents incubate and feed young.
- DAYS TO FLEDGE: Twenty-three to twenty-eight days.

PLACING THE NEST BOX: Place in shade, near sparsely scattered trees, but out of jumping range of squirrels. Face nest boxes south with an open flyway if possible; avoid hot afternoon sun.

- MOUNTING: Mount on trees, metal poles, or wood posts. Tilt box forward about fifteen degrees to make it easier for parents to feed young.
- HEIGHT: Ten to fourteen feet.

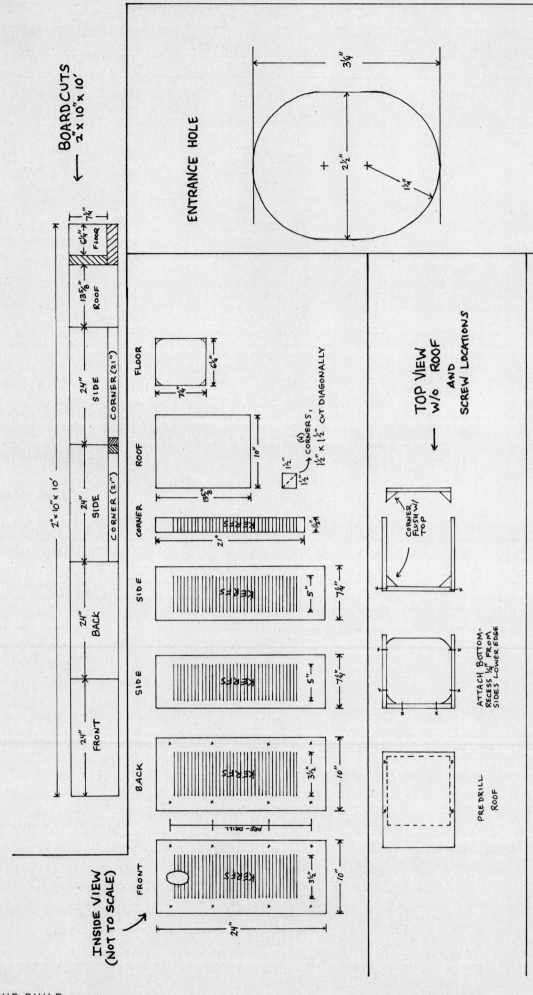

THE BOWER FLICKER BOX

DESIGN: ALLEN BOWER
DRAWN BY: CHRIS WILLETT

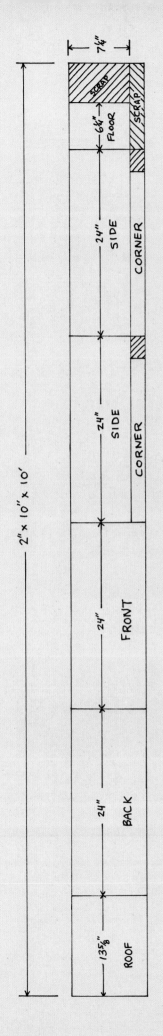

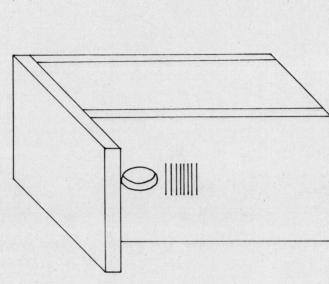

THE BOWER FLICKER BOX

DESIGN BY: ALLEN BOWER

DRAWN BY: CHRIS WILLETT

(NOT TO SCALE)

BOWER FLICKER BOX

DESIGNED BY ALLEN BOWER

1

The four corner pieces are cut from the two side scraps. See drawing. Carefully cut these pieces at a 45 degree angle, using a table saw. Trim each of the four corner pieces to 21".

MATERIALS

- One 2"x10"x10' piece of pine (used here) or Douglas fir (actual size is 1½" thick x 9½")
- Twenty-four 2½" exterior deck screws
- White pine animal bedding (wood shavings)

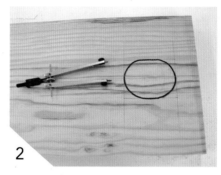

2

To create the 3¼" tall by 2½" wide oval entry hole, mark the oval with pencil lines, then align a drill bit at the top mark and drill the first hole. Next, align the bit with the bottom mark and drill the second hole.

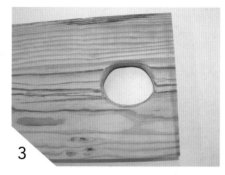

3

Chisel out leftover wood between holes to create the oval. Sand the entry hole smooth.

BEHIND THE DESIGN

Allen Bower's nickname—Flickerman—is well earned. In 1990, the Michigan native saw flickers nesting in a hollow limb of his backyard box elder tree. Curious about the nest site, Bower climbed nearly twenty feet up to it and started measuring. The entry hole was well worn, about two and a half inches wide and three and a quarter inches high. The cavity was eighteen inches deep. From these findings Bower made a flicker nest box, which hatched eight young the first year. Uniquely, his design calls for small cuts or kerfs all around the inside of the box—"just like those made by birds chiseling out a tree cavity." Flickers have returned to his nest boxes nearly every spring. "If the birds are happy," says Bower, "they'll come back." Bower published his research on flicker egg-dumping in *Wilson Bulletin* (March 2004). He is a lifelong member of several bluebird organizations and received a North American Bluebird Society Conservation Award in 2003.

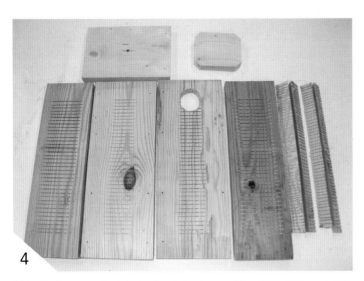

4

Make kerf cuts on the interior front, back, and sides, ½" to ¾" apart, ¼" deep and 3" from all top and bottom edges. As per drawings, make kerf cuts 3½" wide on the center of the front and back and 5" wide on the sides. Make kerf cuts on the angled corner pieces as well. Birds will use the kerf cuts as footholds. Cut ¾" off floor corners for drainage holes.

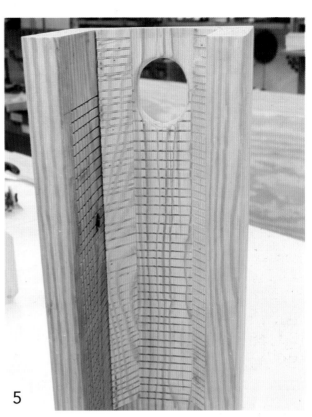

5

Predrill front, back, and roof. Space four holes evenly along each long side of front and back. Predrill roof in four places, ensuring a screw will contact each side. Three of these screws will be removed when checking and cleaning. The fourth will serve as a pivot.

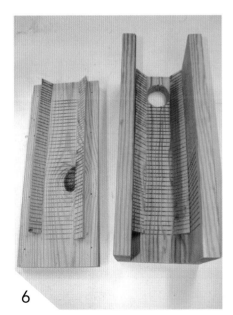

6

Attach two kerf-cut corner pieces to the front with finish nails or small screws. Be sure they are flush with the top of the box to allow drainage to the corners. Install the floor on the three sides. Recess the floor up from the bottom ¼" to prevent water seepage. Nail the remaining two corner pieces to the back piece so that it will fit into the nest cavity of the box (refer to drawing).

7

Assemble the back to the sides using the predrilled holes. Be sure to attach one screw through the back into the floor as well.

8

Attach roof through predrilled holes. Fill the entire nest box with softwood chips. Northern Flickers will "excavate" those chips if they choose your nest box.

Barn Owl   *Tyto alba*

A female Barn Owl in an almond orchard in California's Central Valley. *Steve Simmons*

Year-round

Barn Owls are among the most widespread of all land birds, but they are nonetheless declining over much of North America, particularly in the Midwest. Key factors include loss of nesting sites (such as large, hollow trees and old barns) and development of agricultural fields and grasslands where these owls hunt. Rodenticides kill Barn Owls indirectly, since rodents are their main food. Because they fly near the ground when hunting, these owls are especially susceptible to vehicle collisions.

RANGE: Barn Owls reside across most of the lower forty-eight United States, parts of Hawaii, southern Canada, and much of the world. Adults are nonmigratory.

FIELD MARKS: These midsized, round-headed, long-legged owls are about fourteen inches in length, with a whitish chest and belly, a short, squared-off tail, and a three-foot wingspan. The Barn Owl's dark eyes contrast with its white satellite-dish and heart-shaped face. Nicknames like Ghost Owl and Monkey-faced Owl are descriptive. Females are bigger than males and may be darker.

VOICE: Unlike the hoots of other owls, Barn Owls produce a long, harsh, raspy call. A softer version—or "purring" call—is used in courtship. Barn Owls and their owlets also hiss loudly at nest predators.

FEEDING: On nighttime hunts, Barn Owls fly low over open habitats, using their night vision and remarkable hearing to find prey like rats, mice, voles, gophers, bats, rabbits, and small birds. Their hearing is so keen, they can capture prey in total darkness. Like other owls, prey is swallowed whole; undigested parts are coughed up as pellets. Nesting Barn Owls may cache (store) prey at the nest site to feed young.

THE NEST SITE

If birds are present, nest boxes can boost local populations. Clean out nest boxes in early fall and position them by November. Barn Owls use their nest boxes for winter roosting and may nest in the same box year after year. Avoid using rodenticides and pesticides.

NESTING: Barn Owls nest and roost in existing quiet cavities in hollow trees, cliffs, caves, or human-made structures such as nest boxes, barns, and church steeples. Females create a nest cup of their own shredded pellets.

A female Barn Owl rests with young, eggs, and abundant prey in the larder, courtesy of the male. When these chicks are hungry, a meal will be close by. *Steve Simmons*

Wide open spaces with abundant rodents are perfect settings for Barn Owl nest boxes. *Steve Simmons*

A female Barn Owl stares at the intruding photographer. *Steve Simmons*

Generally monogamous, these owls sometimes produce more than two broods a year.

- **EGGS:** Two to eighteen; average of seven dull white eggs.
- **EGG-LAYING:** Two- to three-day intervals.
- **INCUBATION:** Twenty-nine to thirty-four days; incubating female relies on male for food.
- **DAYS TO FLEDGE:** Fifty to fifty-five days.

PLACING THE NEST BOX: Mount box near hunting grounds, including large open marshes, grasslands, agricultural fields, orchards, and vineyards, far from roads and train tracks. Space boxes at least eighty yards apart. If heat is a problem, plant boxes white.

- **NESTING MATERIALS:** Add three-quarters of an inch of wood shavings to nest box floor.
- **MOUNTING:** Attach to a ten-foot metal pole that's one and a half to two inches wide. Stabilize pole by placing it two feet deep into cement or onto ground socket. Make sure the nest box is level. Can also be mounted on barns and trees.
- **HEIGHT:** Eight to ten feet above ground.

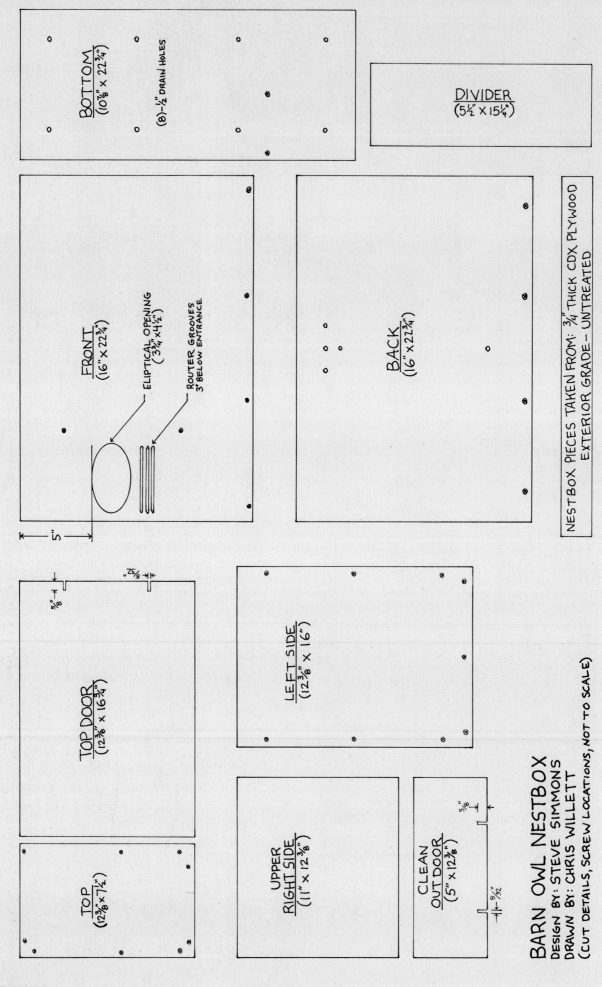

BOTTOM
(10⅞" × 22¾")

(8) - ½" DRAIN HOLES

DIVIDER
(5½" × 15¼")

FRONT
(16" × 22¾")

ELIPTICAL OPENING
(3¾" × 4½")

ROUTER GROOVES
3" BELOW ENTRANCE

5"

BACK
(16" × 22¾")

NESTBOX PIECES TAKEN FROM: ¾" THICK CDX PLYWOOD
EXTERIOR GRADE - UNTREATED

TOP DOOR
(12⅜" × 16¾")

⅝"

5/32"

LEFT SIDE
(12⅜" × 16")

TOP
(12⅜" × 7½")

UPPER
RIGHT SIDE
(11" × 12⅜")

CLEAN
OUT DOOR
(5" × 12⅜")

5/16"

5/32"

BARN OWL NESTBOX
DESIGN BY: STEVE SIMMONS
DRAWN BY: CHRIS WILLETT
(CUT DETAILS, SCREW LOCATIONS, NOT TO SCALE)

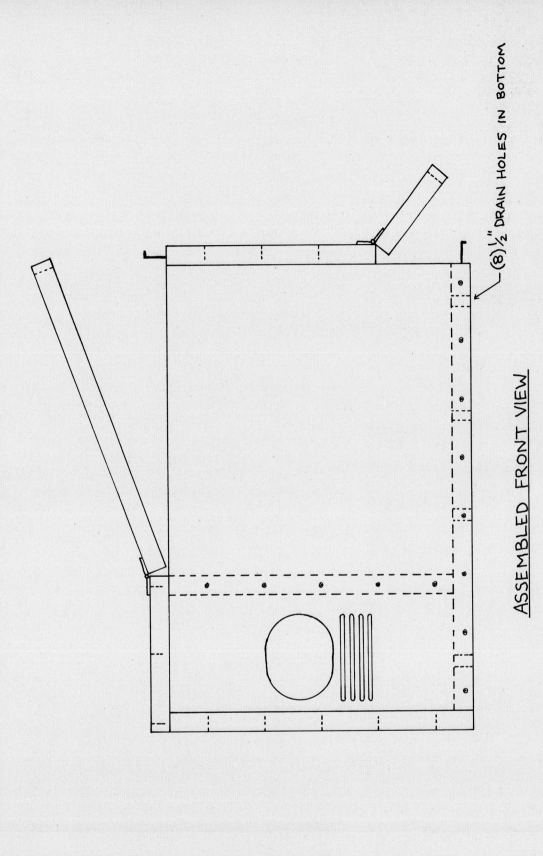

(8) ½" DRAIN HOLES IN BOTTOM

ASSEMBLED FRONT VIEW

BARN OWL NEST BOX
DESIGN BY: STEVE SIMMONS
DRAWN BY: CHRIS WILLETT
(OPERATIONAL VIEW, SCREW LOCATIONS – NOT TO SCALE)

BARN OWL NEST BOX

DESIGNED BY STEVE SIMMONS

MATERIALS

- One sheet of ¾"x4'x8' CDX exterior-grade untreated plywood
- Seventy 1⅝" to 2" exterior No. 8 deck screws
- Four 2" square bend screws or L screws
- Two pairs of hinges 1½x1½" (exterior grade) with hinge screws
- Exterior-grade wood glue, nontoxic variety (Tite-Bond II)
- Two ½" metal flux brushes

QUICK TIP

L screws have a practical advantage over a traditional screw in that a trail monitor need merely twist the L screws about a quarter turn with a pair of pliers to release the door. An additional advantage of L screws over conventional screws is that L screws are never lost in the field, since they are not removed from the box.

QUICK TIP

Glue all pieces before assembly. Attach as soon as possible. An air nailer can quickly "tack" pieces together. This keeps everything in line and square before predrilling. Next, assemble all pieces. Wait until glue has dried before applying any stain. Remove any excess glue with a razor blade, or sand it off.

1

Cut all pieces according to the diagrams. Predrilling is recommended when using plywood. The nest box is put together using No. 8 exterior deck screws and waterproof glue. Predrill 5/32" clearance holes for the screws ⅜" from the edge of the top, front, sides, and back at the spots indicated in the drawings and photos.

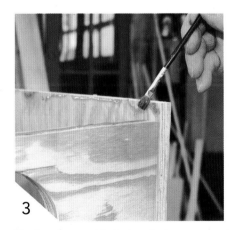

2

Cut out the elliptical entrance hole using a jigsaw. Use a router with a ⅜" straight bit to cut out three or four grip grooves below the entrance hole on the exterior side. Note two slots made in each of the top door and clean-out door pieces. These are for the L screws.

BEHIND THE DESIGN

In four decades of studying birds around California's Central Valley, former high school woodshop teacher Steve Simmons has banded more than 14,000 Barn Owls. He got involved with owls when he and his students turned agricultural waste—damaged plywood prune crates—into simple Barn Owl boxes. As the design evolved, Simmons added an elliptical entry hole to deter raccoons and Great Horned Owls. Another unique "owl-tested" feature is an inside divider that creates two chambers, so predators can't see the young and vice versa. Simmons' nest boxes are popular with farmers and ranchers. "When they learn a family of owls consumes about seventy pounds of rodents in eight weeks, they welcome my nest boxes," says Simmons, adding, "Barn Owls are the best natural pest control around." In 2006, Simmons was named a *Field and Stream* "Heroes of Conservation" finalist for his Wood Duck restoration work.

3

The box is assembled using deck screws (No. 8, 1⅝ to 2" long) and exterior glue. Deck screws are preferred since they are more weather resistant than other screws. Any surface on this box held together with screws should also be glued. Using the small metal brush, coat both surfaces before assembly.

4

Attach the divider to the front. Drill eight ½" diameter drain holes in the floor.

5

Glue together the front, back, and floor.

6

One side is attached to front, back, and floor.

7

Attach the clean-out door using hinges. Insert the clean-out door L-screws (use 3/32" pilot bit).

8

Attach top door with hinges. Insert top door L screws on upper edge of clean-out door side. Use a 3/32" pilot bit. Tighten L screws until snug. If desired, after assembly, finish with low VOC semi-transparent stain.

9

Hang the Barn Owl nest box on a metal pole, a barn, or a tree. This nest box (see page 88) was bolted onto an angle iron frame that was welded to a 1½" diameter metal pole.

American Kestrel

Falco sparverius

A close-up of a captive female American Kestrel. *Paul Spurling, courtesy of the Peregrine Fund/Americana Kestrel Partnership*

Breeding
Breeding and winter
Wintering

From the late nineteenth century until about the mid-1930s, kestrels (formerly called sparrow hawks), along with other birds of prey, were hunted in huge numbers during fall migration.

Today, although the birds are no longer hunted, nesting habitat for American Kestrels can be hard to find. This small falcon hunts in open farmlands and grasslands, yet it favors nest sites like old woodpecker tree cavities and protected rock ledges. Although declining in parts of their range, kestrels accept nest boxes, a practice that helps increase local populations.

RANGE: Breeds throughout North America up into Alaska and northern Canada, and south into Mexico and South America.

FIELD MARKS: The smallest and most colorful falcon in the Americas. The male's pointy wings and large round head are slate-blue, with black vertical lines on a white face, a rusty-red tail and back, black band near the tail tip, and pale undersides. Females

are paler, rustier, and larger. Look for "tail-flicking" when perched and "hover-hunting" in the air.

VOICE: Sharp call is a series of *klee* notes or *killy-killy-killy*.

FEEDING: Hunts in open country for ground-dwelling insects, frogs, snakes, and rodents, especially voles.

This male American Kestrel is on the lookout for prey at the Hawk Mountain Sanctuary in eastern Pennsylvania. Kestrels will stash extra food in bushes, tree limbs, and elsewhere, storing it for future use. *Courtesy of the Hawk Mountain Sanctuary*

HAWK MOUNTAIN SANCTUARY

Photos of a raptor slaughter in 1932 at what was called Hawk Mountain in eastern Pennsylvania caught the attention of conservationist Rosalie Edge. She later bought the property. In time it became Hawk Mountain Sanctuary, the first refuge for birds of prey.

Hawk Mountain Sanctuary curator Alex Nagy helped pioneer nest box use for kestrels in the early 1950s. Today, research at the sanctuary and elsewhere is attempting to identify reasons for recent kestrel declines in New England, the Great Lakes, and California.

Scarcity of nesting sites, prevalence of environmental toxins, predation by raccoons, and in some areas, Cooper's Hawks, may be contributing to these declines.

Keith Bildstein, director of conservation science for the Hawk Mountain Sanctuary, says as many as 5,000 kestrels have been hatched and banded at Hawk Mountain since the nest box program began. "By monitoring kestrels in nest boxes over a long period of time, we have learned much about their breeding, wintering, and migratory habits," he notes.

Seeks prey while perched on utility poles or in hovering flight. Can catch small birds in the air. Ultraviolet vision enables kestrels to see urine trails that may lead to prey, especially voles. Male feeds female during much of the breeding season.

THE NEST SITE

In northern states, set up new nest boxes in early March, before kestrels return. Also check and clean out established nest boxes at that time. Young can be found in the nest as late as August. Nest boxes may also be cleaned out in the fall once nesting season is over. Most kestrels migrate, but some use nest boxes as winter roosting boxes.

NESTING: Male finds nest site such as an old woodpecker hole, rock crevice, or human-built nest box and attracts the female to the site where she makes an oval scrape in existing nest materials or supplied pine wood shavings.

- EGGS: Usually four to five creamy, yellowish, or reddish-brown elliptical eggs with brown, gray, and burgundy splotches. The last egg laid is usually lightest in color.

Two spots at the back of the kestrel's neck, called "eyespots," resemble large eyes to startle intruders. This female is raising four downy chicks, about ten days old.
Richard M. Tuttle

- **EGG-LAYING:** About one egg every other day. The clutch is usually completed within nine days.
- **INCUBATION:** The female incubates about thirty days; hatching takes three to four days. The female then broods nestlings for about ten days.
- **DAYS TO FLEDGE:** Twenty-eight to thirty-one days. The young depend on parents for two weeks after fledging, returning to the nest at night to roost.

PLACEMENT: Open country, such as farmland, near grassy foraging areas and perches. Because kestrels can prey on small birds, do not locate kestrel boxes near bird feeders or nonkestrel nest boxes. Also avoid placing boxes near woods where Cooper's and other bird-eating hawks can prey on young kestrels.

- **NESTING MATERIALS:** Place two to three inches of small pine wood chips or small animal bedding on the nest box floor to cushion the kestrel eggs.
- **MOUNTING:** Nest boxes have been successfully attached to stop signs, barns, or electric company utility poles (with written permission from the utility company). Wrap long aluminum flashing, at least twenty inches wide, around utility poles just under the nest boxes. Winches, pulley systems, ropes, straps, and carabiners all can help to safely raise and lower kestrel boxes.
- **SPACING:** At least a half mile from other kestrel nesting sites.
- **HEIGHT:** Eight to thirty feet high.

This kestrel nest box hangs on a freestanding pole; a winch will bring it safely to the ground for nest checking and cleaning. This nest box is located in great kestrel habitat—wide-open views all around, perches galore, and plenty of space to hunt. *Richard M. Tuttle*

BEHIND THE DESIGN

Retired science teacher Dick Tuttle of Ohio's Delaware County Bird Club spent forty-plus years on bluebird nest box projects. He was the first education director for the North American Bluebird Society. Tuttle's bird world expanded in the mid-1990s to include American Kestrels. He currently makes fifty-mile rounds with fellow teacher Dick Phillips to check eighteen kestrel nest boxes, most on utility poles. The 2012 season produced record numbers of kestrels. Tuttle's unique kestrel nest box design features decoy entry holes on the sides, which help encourage kestrels to explore the nest box and choose "this" one. Another design feature is a hinged rooftop opening, which enables quick, safe nest checking. "Top-down peeking greatly reduces the chance of spooking the birds," says Tuttle. "They might be annoyed by our visits, but by-and-large, we lift up the lid, get our data, lower the lid, and the birds stay in the box." Spurred to educate others about America's smallest falcon, Tuttle's motto is "Raptor on!" In 2009, Dick Tuttle received Columbus Audubon's Song Sparrow Award for his work helping cavity-nesting birds.

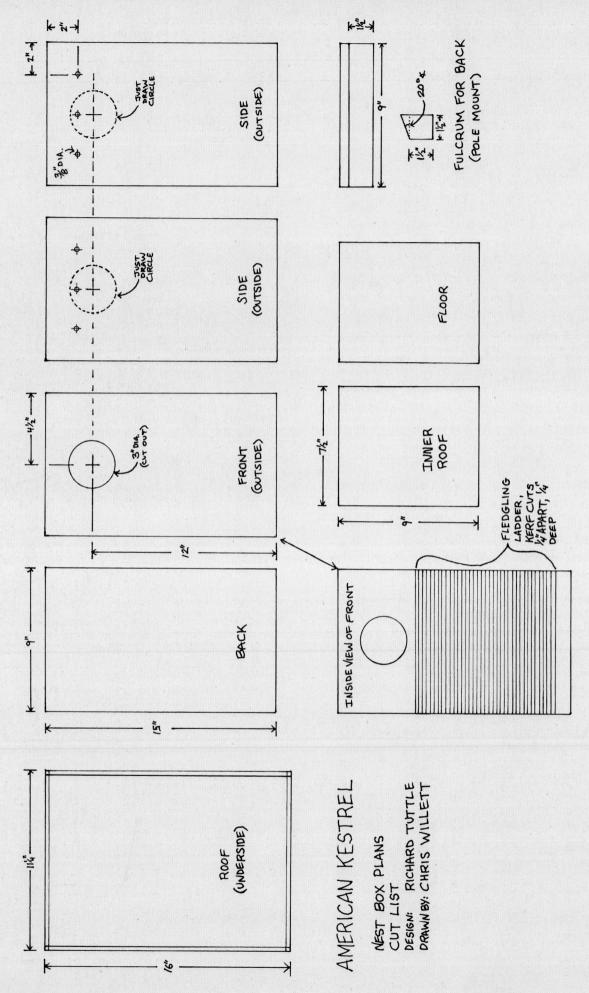

AMERICAN KESTREL

NEST BOX PLANS
CUT LIST
DESIGN: RICHARD TUTTLE
DRAWN BY: CHRIS WILLETT

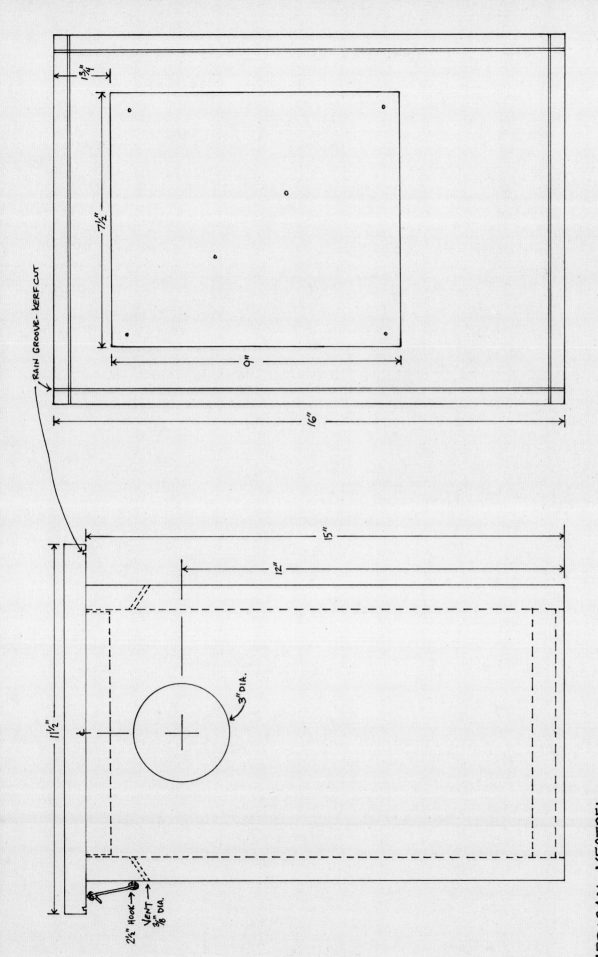

RAIN GROOVE- KERF CUT

1 3/4"

7 1/2"

9"

16"

15"

12"

11 1/2"

3" DIA.

¢

2 1/2" HOOK

VENT
3/8" DIA.

AMERICAN KESTREL

NEST BOX PLANS / FRONT AND ROOF VIEWS
DESIGN: RICHARD TUTTLE
DRAWN BY: CHRIS WILLETT

AMERICAN KESTREL NEST BOX

DESIGN BY DICK TUTTLE

MATERIALS

- One 1x12x16" pine (used here), cypress, or cedar
- One 1"x10"x 8' pine (used here), cypress, or cedar
- About thirty 2½" exterior grade decking screws
- Six 1¼" exterior grade deck screws
- Two 3" galvanized strap hinges
- One hook and eye closure

1

Cut all pieces according to the list specifications. Sand pieces to remove sharp edges. Sand the inner roof piece enough that it will fit into the nest chamber and allow for some expansion due to humidity.

2

Lay out the entrance hole and two decoy holes. Only one hole should be cut or drilled out; the others can just be marked. Make sure they are all at the same level from the top.

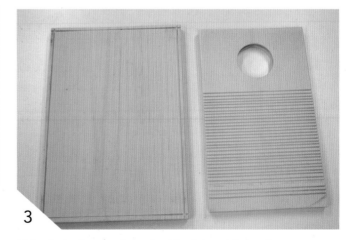

3

Make the kerf cut on the underside of the roof piece for water diversion. Make a ³⁄₁₆"-deep cut around the perimeter of the underside of roof piece ⅜" from edge. Be sure the crown is down to allow the proper warping of the wood over time. Inside the front piece, or entrance hole piece, make the fledgling ladder by cutting horizontal kerfs ³⁄₁₆" deep every ¼ to ½". Start the cuts approximately 1" from the bottom and continue to just under the entrance hole. Just like the rungs on a ladder, this helps the fledgling to reach the entrance hole.

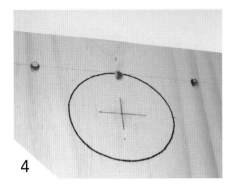

4

Mark three vent holes on what is considered the exterior of each of the two sides. Locate the vents 1½" down from the top. The two end vents are 2" from the edge. Place the center vent midway between them. Drill all six vents with a ⅜" bit at a slightly upward angle. This angle helps prevent intrusion of water in high wind and rain.

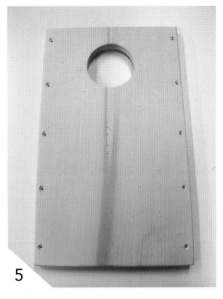

5

Start the assembly by predrilling the front and back pieces. There will be five screws per each long edge of the front and back. Starting from the bottom edge, make a mark at approximately 1", 4¼", 7½", 10¾", and at 14"; these will all be ⅜" in from the edge. Predrill those locations.

6

Predrill the inner roof piece as well, one hole at each corner approximately ¾" in and two near the center. Center the inner roof piece and place it 1¾" from the back edge. Attach the inner roof to the top roof piece using 1¼" screws.

7

Assemble the nest chamber by attaching the front to the sides, then the back to the sides using 2" exterior grade screws in the predrilled locations. Be sure all edges are tight and even.

8

Install the bottom piece. Be sure to recess the floor ⅜" from the bottom edge, to reduce the risk of water infiltration. Predrill and install using 2" screws per sides.

9

Attach the roof to the front by placing the inner roof (which is attached to the main roof piece) into the nest chamber. Using two strap hinges (zinc coated is preferred for durability), secure into place. Be certain the hinges are attached to the front of the box above the entrance hole so that the back is what lifts off. Install hook and eye closure. The eye is left of the vent near the back and the hook is above it, under the roof.

10

Finish the exterior with a low-to-no VOC exterior water-based semi-transparent solid color stain. Do *not* stain any interior areas. It is especially important to give the roof a few extra coats, as this is the most exposed part of the box.

11

Allow the stain to completely dry, and then paint the decoy holes marked earlier with a flat exterior black paint.

12

To hang the American Kestrel nest box on a utility pole (see page 96), drill two holes in the sides near the fulcrum. String a vinyl-coated wire rope through the holes. Make a loop, clasp it, and hang over lag bolt or roofing nail. Attach a bolt snap hook to the ends of the wire rope for easy box removal.

Black-capped Chickadee   *Poecile atricapilla*

Year-round

A Black-capped Chickadee sings a spring song at Queen's University Biological Station in eastern Ontario—a strong, clear *fee-bee*. *Dan Mennill*

Carolina Chickadee   *Poecile carolinensis*

Year-round

Insects like this small green caterpillar provide protein for Black-capped and other chickadees during the breeding season. Chickadees also eat black-oil sunflower seeds at feeders all year long. *Ashok Khosla*

Mountain Chickadee

Poecile gambeli

Year-round

Chickadee identification gets tricky when the distinctive white stripe above the Mountain Chickadee's eyes wears away to black. From April into August, the three chickadee species look much alike. *Ashok Kholsa*

Seven chickadee species can be found in North America. The closely related Black-capped, Carolina, and Mountain Chickadees are the most widespread. Due in part to these diminutive birds' remarkable adaptations for thriving in extreme weather, chickadee populations are doing well. Some forest fragmentation can benefit chickadees by increasing forest edge, but deforestation eliminates tree stumps that chickadees excavate for nesting. House Wrens and mice are also formidable nest site competitors.

RANGE: The nonmigratory Black-capped Chickadee is found coast to coast, throughout the northern two-thirds of the United States up into Alaska and Canada. Carolina Chickadees reside in the southeastern United States but are expanding northward. Mountain Chickadees live in the high-elevation coniferous forests of southern Arizona, Baja California, British Columbia, and the Yukon. Where these species overlap, they may hybridize.

FIELD MARKS: The five-inch-long Black-capped Chickadee has a wingspan of eight inches, a relatively long tail, black cap and bib, and large, white cheek patches. Carolina Chickadees are slightly smaller than the other two species. Mountain Chickadees sport a seasonal white stripe over the eyes.

VOICE: All three chickadees produce a *chick-a-dee-dee-dee* or dee-dee-dee call with slight variations. The Black-capped Chickadee sings a clear, plaintive *fee-be-be* or *fee-bee*, with the first note higher. Carolina sings three to five varying notes of *see bee see bay*. Mountain Chickadee songs are longer than Black-capped's.

FEEDING: Chickadees survive cold winters by gathering insects, seeds, and berries, consuming as many calories by day as they lose by night. Black-capped Chickadees may cache hundreds of seeds daily and remember cache locations for weeks. Although conspicuous at feeders, feeder foods comprise only one-fifth of the chickadees' diet. In warm weather, chickadees consume large amounts of insects and spiders.

THE NEST SITE

Feeders stocked with black oil sunflower seeds and suet can enhance chickadee survival. Planting willow, alder, and birch trees provides future nesting habitat. Chickadees also use nest "starts" to excavate nesting cavities; help them by drilling (one and one-eighth inches wide) starts in dead forest trees. Nest boxes or artificial "tree snags" made from wood or PVC tubes are likely to be accepted by all seven chickadee species, especially

BEHIND THE DESIGN

In the mid-1990s, Ohio State University researchers Tom Grubb and Cindy Bronson began studies of central Ohio's chickadees by testing artificial nesting structures they called "snags." These snags were ten-foot-tall, four-inch-diameter PVC tubes that became known as "Grubb stakes." Ten years later, researchers at the Cornell Lab of Ornithology wondered if upstate New York chickadees might prefer these PVC snags over typical square wooden nest boxes. They were right. Three seasons of data showed chickadees nested more often in wood-chip–filled snags than in boxes. Chickadees may like the snag design for its entrance hole, which is high up and less accessible to mice and predators. Canadian chickadee researchers Ken Otter and Daniel Mennill shortened the Grubb stake to about fourteen inches for easier use in the field. In response to environmental concerns over PVC, as well as moisture levels inside the vinyl tube, woodworker Chris Willett created a wooden version of the shortened snag, which is currently under review by the chickadees.

where natural nest sites are rare. Mount nest boxes by early February in the south and by April elsewhere, and fill boxes with wood chips up to the entry hole before breeding season begins. Chickadees may also use bluebird nest boxes. Clean out nest boxes in the fall and spring. Chickadees also use nest boxes for roosting during cold winter nights.

NESTING: Both parents excavate a six- to eight-inch-deep nest cavity in a tree snag or use abandoned woodpecker holes or nest boxes. The nest, made of moss, pine needles and strips of bark, can fill the entire cavity; it is lined with softer plant fibers and animal hair.

- EGGS: Usually six to eight, but range from five to ten white eggs with reddish spots.
- EGG-LAYING: One egg per day, in the morning.

- INCUBATION: Eleven to thirteen days. Female incubates; both parents feed chicks.
- DAYS TO FLEDGE: Fourteen to eighteen days after hatching.

PLACING THE NEST BOX: Place artificial snags or nest boxes in shady areas in woodlands with open spaces; suburban locales are acceptable as well.

- NESTING MATERIALS: Fill nest box with wood chips up to the level of the entrance.
- MOUNTING: Hang on a metal or wooden pole with predator guards. Hanging directly on a favorite chickadee tree, with predator guards, may also increase nesting success.
- HEIGHT: Hang at heights that permit easy checking.

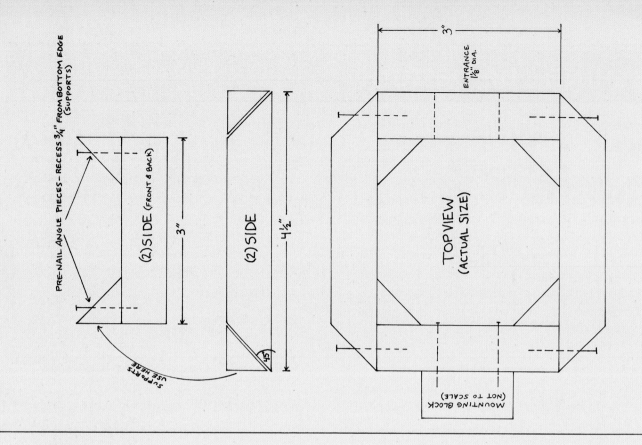

PRE-NAIL ANGLE PIECES — RECESS ¾" FROM BOTTOM EDGE (SUPPORTS)

(2) SIDE (FRONT & BACK)

3"

(2) SIDE

4½"

45°

SUPPORTS USE HERE

TOP VIEW (ACTUAL SIZE)

3"

ENTRANCE 1⅛" DIA.

MOUNTING BLOCK (NOT TO SCALE)

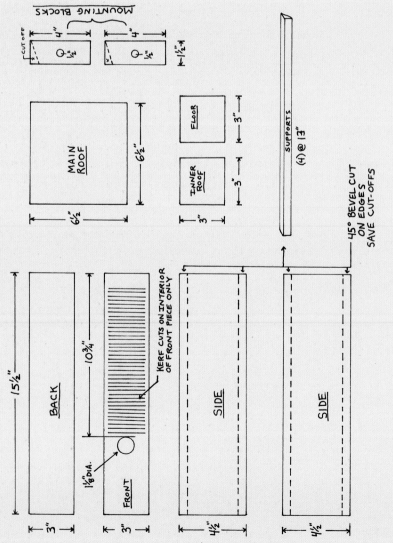

MOUNTING BLOCKS

CUT OFF

4"   4"

Ø-½"   Ø-½"

1½"

MAIN ROOF

6½"

6½"

FLOOR

3"

3"

INNER ROOF

3"

3"

SUPPORTS

(4) @ 13"

45° BEVEL CUT ON EDGES SAVE CUT-OFFS

BACK

15½"

3"

10¾"

1⅛" DIA.

FRONT

3"

KERF CUTS ON INTERIOR OF FRONT PIECE ONLY

SIDE

4½"

SIDE

4½"

CHICKADEE NEST BOX

DESIGNED AND DRAWN BY: CHRIS WILLETT

(CUT VIEW AND ASSEMBLY VIEW)

(NOT TO SCALE)

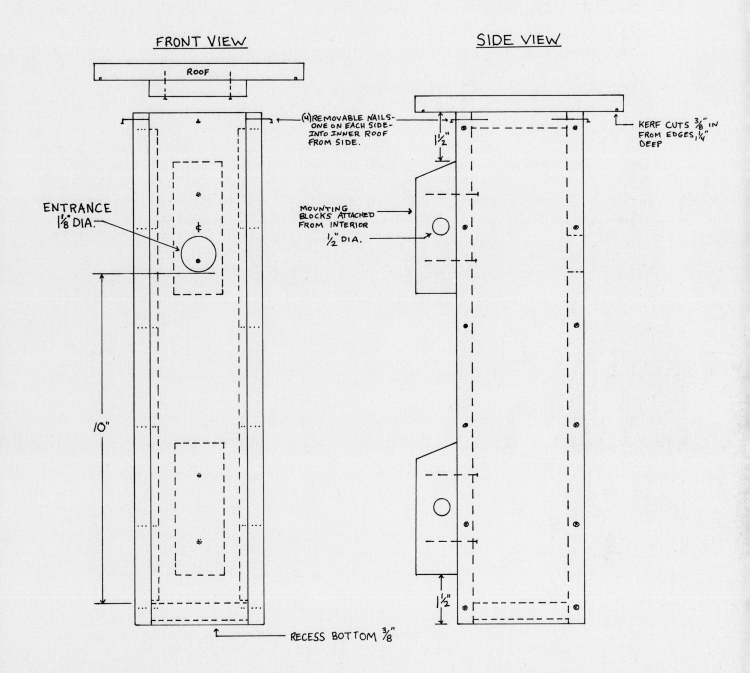

FRONT VIEW

SIDE VIEW

ROOF

ENTRANCE 1⅛" DIA.

(4) REMOVABLE NAILS-
ONE ON EACH SIDE-
INTO INNER ROOF
FROM SIDE.

KERF CUTS ⅜" IN
FROM EDGES, ¼"
DEEP

MOUNTING
BLOCKS ATTACHED
FROM INTERIOR
½" DIA.

1½"

10"

1½"

RECESS BOTTOM ⅜"

CHICKADEE NEST BOX
DESIGNED AND DRAWN BY: CHRIS WILLETT
(SCREW LOCATIONS, LAYOUT, ASSEMBLED VIEWS)
(NOT TO SCALE)

CHICKADEE NEST BOX

DESIGNED BY CHRIS WILLETT
BASED ON THE RESEARCH OF KEN OTTER AND DANIEL MENNILL

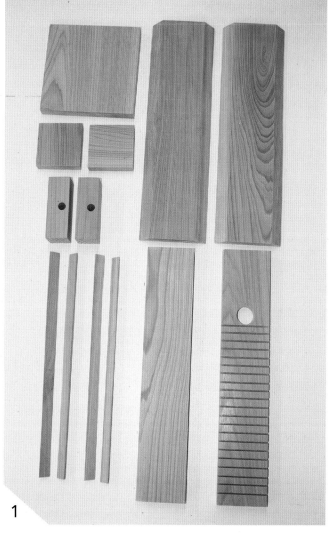

1

Cut out thirteen pieces total. Predrill mounting blocks with ½" diameter holes. On front piece, make ¼" deep kerf cuts on front interior, ⅜" from edges, every ½" (from bottom to just below entry hole). Cut from the sides, four interior corner supports (45-degree cutoffs), creating four beveled edges. Trim supports to 13" each. Predrill to avoid splitting wood, and countersink all screws. Refer to drawing.

MATERIALS

- One 1x4x37¼" cypress board
- One 1x6x31¼" cypress board
- One 2x4x4" cypress board
- One 1x8x6½" cypress board
- Thirty 2" exterior-grade deck screws
- Four 1¼" exterior-grade deck screws (used to attach inner roof to the main roof)
- Three 2½" galvanized finish nails (bend heads 90 degrees for latch nail)
- Optional light-colored, water-based exterior stain
- Air-nailer with 1" brads (hand nails will also work)

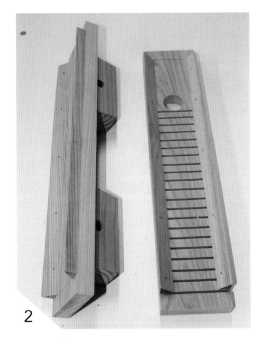

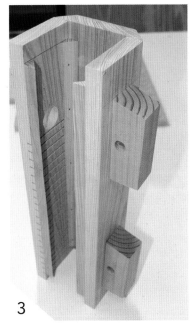

2

Place inner supports ¾" below the top edge of the front and back (space for inner roof) and 1" up from the bottom (space for recessed floor). With an air-nailer, attach supports with 1" brads or use small 1" hand nails. The corners create a rounded effect in the nest chamber.

3

Before assembly of the nest chamber, attach the mounting blocks from what will be the inside of the nest chamber through the back piece (use four 2½" screws on each—and predrill).

4

Assemble the nest chamber by predrilling and attaching the sides to the front and back. Refer to the drawing.

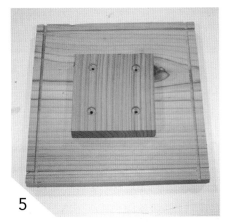

5

With the crown down, make kerf cuts on the underside of the main roof piece (⅜" in from all edges, ¼" deep). Mark where the inner roof will be attached: equal distance from the outside edges. Predrill carefully. *Do not* go all the way through the main roof. Use 1¼" screws to attach the inner roof to the main. Set the inner roof into the nest chamber. It may have to be sanded slightly to fit. Make a distinguishing mark toward the front: This will aide with aligning the roof in the future. Use a ⅛" drill bit and drill through the two sides and the front into the inner roof. These holes will accommodate the bent-head galvanized-finish nails, which will secure the roof to the nest chamber. Install the floor with 2" screws. Be sure to predrill and to recess the floor approximately ⅜" from bottom. The floor piece may have to be sanded slightly to fit. Optional: two to four ¼" drain holes in the floor.

6

Latch nails make roof removal easy. Thread vinyl-coated wire rope through mounting blocks and attach clasps. Opposite page: this chickadee nest box is attached to a paper birch tree, a chickadee favorite.

Wood Duck

Aix sponsa

Male and female Wood Ducks often swim and "house hunt" together. Where a nest box is available, they will check it out in tandem. *Ashok Khosla*

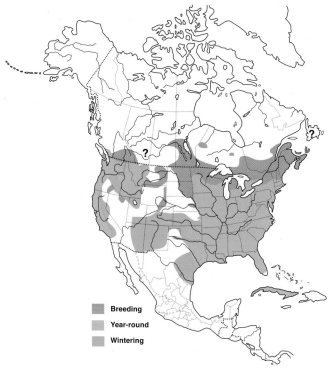

Breeding

Year-round

Wintering

Close-up details of a male Wood Duck's spectacular plumage. *Ashok Khosla*

These colorful ducks of forested wetlands were over-harvested for food and feathers throughout the nineteenth century. The Wood Duck's steep decline was hastened by the draining of wetlands for development and harvesting of mature timber. Although this species is still hunted, bird-protection laws, hunting restrictions, and the use of nest boxes have helped it rebound.

RANGE: Wood Ducks are permanent residents in much of their southern and northwestern breeding range; they migrate south from more northern breeding grounds.

FIELD MARKS: Breeding males have a purple-green iridescent head, long crest, red eyes, and ornate white stripes on the head, neck, and body. Females are gray-brown with white patches around the eyes. Wood Ducks average twenty inches long with a twenty-seven-inch wingspan and are recognizable in flight by long, rectangle-shaped tails (which they use as a woodpecker-like prop when clinging to their nest trees). Although most often seen on water, these sharp-clawed ducks can fly through forests and perch on trees.

VOICE: The male's whistles are a rising and falling *jeeb*. The female's whistle calls of *oo-eeek*, *oo-eek* are often made when the duck is disturbed or taking flight.

FEEDING: The omnivorous Wood Duck feeds in water or on land, eating nuts, seeds, fruits, and aquatic insects. Wood Ducks can be found in fields eating corn and in forests feeding on acorns, a favorite food.

More than one Wood Duck hen has been laying eggs in this nest box—a process known as "egg dumping."
Aaron Ward, courtesy of the Maryland Wood Duck Society

A female Wood Duck settles into a nest made from her own down feathers. *Steve Simmons*

THE NEST SITE

Egg-laying can begin in late January in the South. In the North, birds return when the ice melts; egg-laying begins soon afterward. Inspect and clean Wood Duck nest boxes before and after breeding season.

NESTING: Wood Ducks seek out hollow trees, old woodpecker holes, or nest boxes for nesting. Females select the nest site. Males guard females until eggs are near hatching. Southern Wood Ducks can produce two broods per year.

- EGGS: Typically six to fifteen white, tan, or olive eggs. Unusually large clutches—as many as forty eggs—consist of eggs deposited or "dumped" by other Wood Duck hens, Hooded Mergansers, or Common Goldeneyes.
- EGG LAYING: One per day.
- INCUBATION: Twenty-eight days. More if large clutch. Females incubate and tend young.
- DAYS TO FLEDGE: One day after hatching, on "Jump Day," a mother Wood Duck calls to the young below the nest box. Chicks then leap and glide from nest to the ground or into water, sometimes dozens of feet down. The female leads ducklings to water to swim and feed. Flight occurs at two months.

PLACING THE NEST BOX: Wooded swamps, marshes, streams, beaver ponds, and small lakes are ideal. Place the nest box where entry flyway is clear, in or near fresh water, but away from trees. If placed on land, face the entry hole toward water.

Male Wood Ducks are characterized by their spectacular coloration. This male cruises over a lake near Cincinnati, Ohio. *Ruhikana Meetei*

- NESTING MATERIALS: Add four inches of wood chips. The hen makes a cup-like depression for the eggs and lines the nest with her own soft down feathers.
- MOUNTING: Place nest boxes on sturdy poles such as eight-foot-long metal highway signposts or four-by-four-inch wooden posts with a predator cone below the nest box. Space nest boxes fifty feet apart.
- HEIGHT: On land, place nest box six feet high. In water, place nest box three feet above historic high water levels.

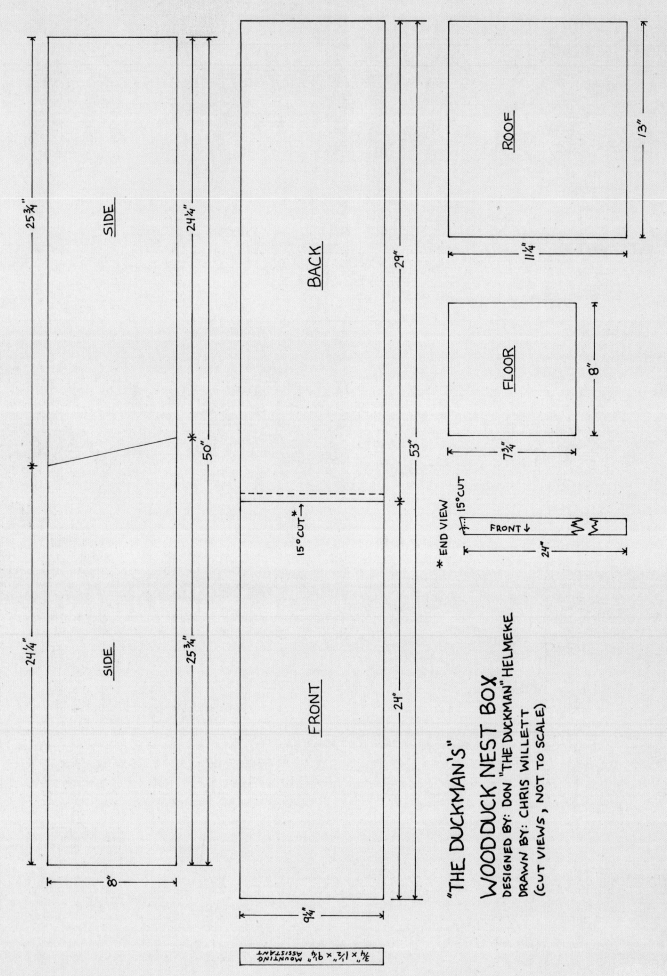

SIDE

SIDE

25¾"

24¼"

24¼"

25¾"

8"

8"

BACK

FRONT

50"

15° CUT *

29"

53"

24"

9¼"

¾" x 1½ x 9¼" MOUNTING ASSISTANT

ROOF

11¼"

13"

FLOOR

7¾"

8"

* END VIEW

15° CUT

FRONT ↓

24"

"THE DUCKMAN'S"
WOODDUCK NEST BOX

DESIGNED BY: DON "THE DUCKMAN" HELMEKE
DRAWN BY: CHRIS WILLETT
(CUT VIEWS, NOT TO SCALE)

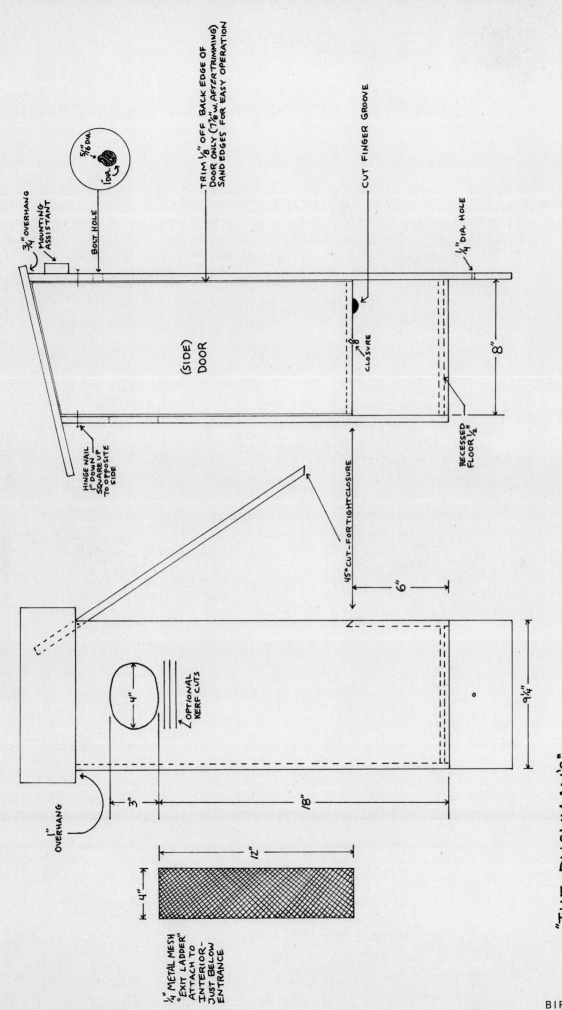

5/16" DIA.
1" DIA.

BOLT HOLE

3/4" OVERHANG

MOUNTING ASSISTANT

TRIM 1/8" OFF BACK EDGE OF DOOR ONLY (7 7/8" W. AFTER TRIMMING) SAND EDGES FOR EASY OPERATION

CUT FINGER GROOVE

1/4" DIA. HOLE

(SIDE) DOOR

8"

CLOSURE

HINGE NAIL (1" DOWN SQUARE UP TO OPPOSITE SIDE

RECESSED FLOOR 1/2"

45° CUT — FOR TIGHT CLOSURE

6"

OPTIONAL KERF CUTS

4"

9 1/4"

o

1" OVERHANG

3"

18"

12"

4"

1/4" METAL MESH "EXIT LADDER" ATTACH TO INTERIOR — JUST BELOW ENTRANCE

"THE DUCKMAN'S"
WOOD DUCK NEST BOX

DESIGNED BY: DON "THE DUCKMAN" HELMEKE

DRAWN BY: CHRIS WILLETT

(OPERATIONAL VIEW. NOT TO SCALE)

DON "THE DUCKMAN'S" WOOD DUCK NEST BOX

DESIGNED BY DON HELMEKE

1

Cut out all the pieces according to the drawing.

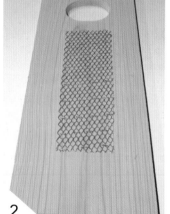

2

Mark the entrance (an elliptical hole 3" high x 4" wide) and cut it out. Attach the 4x12" metal mesh to interior of the front piece with a staple gun about 1" below the entry hole. Be certain there are no sharp edges protruding, which can hurt the adults and youngsters alike.

3

Start attaching front and back pieces to side and floor, as shown. Check angle at top of side to ensure proper roof alignment. Install floor and recess it ½" from bottom edges. Drain holes are not used in this design.

MATERIALS

- One 1"x10"x10' cypress (used here) or cedar
- One 1x12x13" cypress (used here) or cedar
- Thirty-five to forty 2" exterior-grade deck screws
- One galvanized screen door "propeller" latch
- One 4x12" wire mesh (¼") or metal lathe (for fledgling exit ladder)

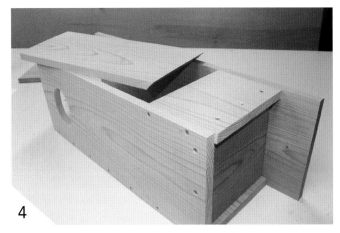

4

Make a 45-degree angle cut in second side, 6" from the bottom. The longer piece will be a pivoted door. The angle keeps out water when door is closed. Test-fit these pieces. Affix smaller side piece through front and back. Screw into floor.

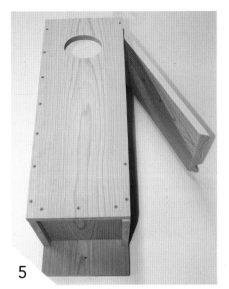

5

Sand the edges on the top portion of the door so it will operate nicely. Mark the location using a square 1" down from the top of the front piece and transfer the mark to the opposite side. Put the door in so that it closes tightly with the 45-degree cut. Drill the holes for the pivot screws, install two deck screws, and see how it works. Adjust if needed.

6

Using a wood rasp, make a finger groove so that the door can be opened easily. Install the "propeller closure." Refer to the drawing.

7

Install the roof. Overhang is largest on front, ¾" off the back, and 1" on each side. Predrill and screw the roof into place. Be certain to not screw into the door side of the box.

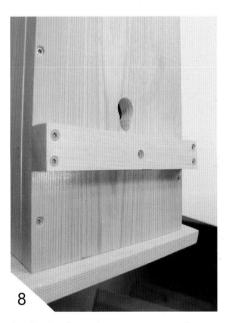

8

A ¾" strip of wood serves as a mounting support. The nest box can be hung onto a pre-positioned lag screw through the keyhole.

BEHIND THE DESIGN

In the 1980s, the late Don Helmeke, a Minnesota outdoorsman and conservationist, worked long and thoughtfully on Wood Duck nest box plans. His design has withstood the test of time. Its success at creating a "safe haven" for nesting birds led to its recommendation by both the Minnesota Waterfowl Association and the Wood Duck Society. "It's a woodworking design that makes sense," says Wood Duck Society director Roger Strand. "The low height—just 6 feet from the ground—and Don's side opening makes for easy, ladder-free nest checking and less disturbance to the hen." Another bonus: "Kids can get nose-to-nose with eggs, which creates a fun learning experience."

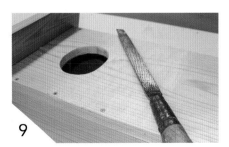

9

Wood Ducks will welcome a kerf cut ladder or a rough surface made by a rasp, just below the entry hole.

Hooded Merganser

Lophodytes cucullatus

A female Hooded Merganser in her element. *Ashok Khosla*

Sexual dimorphism is apparent in male (left) and female (right) Hooded Mergansers. *Ashok Khosla*

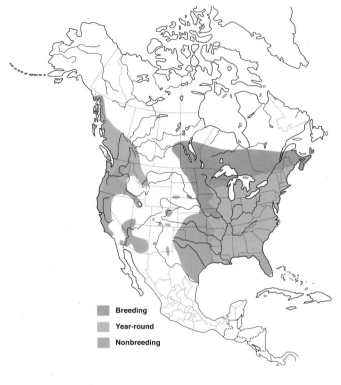

Breeding

Year-round

Nonbreeding

Hooded Mergansers are fairly common on small ponds, rivers, and streams, with stable populations across their breeding range. This species was overhunted in the early to mid-twentieth century; simultaneously, logging and alteration of many forests where they nested reduced breeding populations. Fortunately, Hooded Mergansers take readily to nest boxes and are often found in nest boxes built for Wood Ducks. Reduced hunting and restoration programs in several states have increased local populations.

RANGE: Hooded Mergansers breed in forested wetlands throughout the eastern half of North America and the Pacific Northwest. They are resident to medium-distance migrants.

FIELD MARKS: These small ducks have long, rounded tails, thin bills, and heads that appear oversized due to the fan-shaped crest on top. Adult males are black above, with a white breast and chestnut flanks. Their black head has a prominent large white patch that expands when the crest is raised, usually during courtship. Females and immatures are gray-brown with a yellow bill and dark eyes; their cinnamon-colored heads also have a distinctive crest. Their legs are set far back on their bodies, which makes them awkward on land. They fly with shallow, rapid wing beats.

VOICE: Hooded Mergansers are usually silent, but during courtship, males make a deep, frog-like sound, and females produce a hoarse *gack*. Females calling in flight or to newly hatched ducklings produce a rough *croo-croo-crook*.

FEEDING: Hooded Mergansers dive and locate their prey underwater by sight. Prey includes aquatic insects, crayfish, amphibians, mollusks, and small fish, which the birds seize with their serrated bills.

THE NEST SITE

Property owners can improve habitat for nesting Hooded Mergansers by leaving dead trees standing and by stocking ponds with shiners and fat-headed minnows. Well-placed, appropriately sized nest boxes, too, can help boost local populations, particularly if sited near wetlands.

The male Hooded Merganser on the left is displaying his showy head crest. *Ashok Khosla*

A Hooded Merganser hen has repurposed an old squirrel's nest. Hooded Merganser eggs are unusually round, like ping pong balls with thick shells.
Aaron Ward, courtesy of the Maryland Wood Duck Initiative

NESTING: In summer, these small ducks nest in cavities, either in live or dead trees, often near freshwater ponds or rivers. Females choose the nest site and create a shallow bowl within existing nesting material, adding their own down once egg-laying begins. Like other cavity-nesting ducks, female Hooded Mergansers may exhibit "egg dumping"—laying their eggs in other females' nests.

- **EGGS:** Five to thirteen white, nearly spherical eggs; single brood
- **EGG-LAYING:** One egg every other day.

- **INCUBATION:** Twenty-six to forty-one days; female incubates
- **DAYS TO FLEDGE:** Day-old ducklings leap more than fifty feet to the forest floor, then walk with their mother to the nearest body of water.

PLACING THE NEST BOX: Mergansers breed in forested wetlands but may also nest in treeless wetlands where nest boxes have been placed.

- **NESTING MATERIALS:** Small amounts of wood chips
- **MOUNTING:** Place nest boxes on sturdy poles such as eight-foot-long metal highway signposts or four-by-four-inch wooden posts with a predator cone below the nest box. Space nest boxes fifty feet apart.
- **HEIGHT:** On land, six feet high. In water, place nest box three feet above historic high water levels.

THE BUILD

Hooded Mergansers will nest in a Wood Duck nest box: see pages 108–109 for plans.

Purple Martin

Progne subis

This glossy Purple Martin male holds tight to his insect prey as he surveys his northern Alabama territory. *Chuck Abare*

A female Purple Martin returns to her plastic "gourd" house with a beak full of dragonfly. *Chuck Abare*

Breeding

Most Purple Martin populations west of the Rockies still nest in woodpecker holes or natural cavities like rock crevices. Others in the Pacific Northwest have begun to nest in gourds and single-room nest boxes, especially over water; however, in eastern North America, where most martins occur, martins have become totally dependent on human-provided housing, either in multifamily martin houses or in natural or plastic gourds. Today, martins returning to nest in the East face competition from nonnative species. At summer's end, martins gather in spectacularly huge flocks in preparation for the long trip back to their South American wintering grounds. Protecting these wintering grounds, including Brazil's Amazon region, is one key to this species' survival.

RANGE: After wintering in South America, Purple Martins slowly spread throughout their North American breeding range, from Florida up into Canada.

FIELD MARKS: The largest swallows in North America, Purple Martins are about eight inches long with an eighteen-inch wingspan. Long, pointed wings let these aerial acrobats flap, soar, and glide in circles. Their large, wide triangular mouths are good for catching flying insects. Males acquire their all-over iridescent blue-black, purplish plumage in their second year. Female adults are gray-purple above, with purple iridescence and lighter gray undersides.

VOICE: Males produce a low-whistled call and a low, rich gurgling song. Male "dawn song" consists of seven to nine notes uttered while flying high above the colony or perched nearby. Western martin calls are higher pitched.

FEEDING: Martins forage from the air by day on a variety of flying insects. Dragonflies are a favorite food. Contrary to conventional wisdom, apparently the result of a marketing campaign decades ago by martin house manufacturers, martins do not consume huge numbers of mosquitoes.

BEHIND THE DESIGN

The *Audubon Birdhouse Book* features Alabama computer designer and Purple Martin landlord Chuck Abare's Simple Wooden Gourd Rack design. While traveling for his job in the mid-1980s, Abare met a Tennessee man who introduced him to Purple Martins. From the get-go, Abare was amazed at the birds' flying skills and wanted to help them survive on their breeding grounds. Learning that Purple Martins are dependent on humans for housing, he set out to build houses and provide colonies with natural and plastic gourds that martins could trust as good homes. "Martins seem to know you are there to help," Abare says. "Giving them good, safe homes is a real way to show them you care."

People have been making gourd birdhouses to attract martins for a long time. Centuries ago, martins in North America nested in hollowed-out gourds provided by Native Americans. These first Americans hung clusters of gourds in trees near their gardens.

The relationship between Purple Martins and humans is mutually beneficial. Humans provide the nest sites; martins provide the cheery calls and purple-sheened sightings so welcome in many backyard gardens. As an added benefit, they eat lots of flying insects. A variety of Purple Martin houses and plastic gourd options are commercially available, but some martin fans prefer to save money by creating homes out of natural gourds or even growing their own gourds.

Whether a swinging gourd cluster is better for a martin colony than a multifamily martin house depends largely upon the house and gourd in question. A "good gourd" is certainly better than a "bad house" and vice versa. Martin gourds need to be relatively large and thick, at least nine inches in diameter, with walls at least one-quarter-inch thick. Southwestern gourds tend to better fit this description, since the growing season there is longer. Today, the consensus among martin experts is that gourds that are properly sized, dried, cleaned, prepared, and maintained, make excellent martin homes—with the added advantage of being completely biodegradable, naturally beautiful, and affordable.

For detailed instructions, visit Abare's website, chuckspurplemartinpage.com.

A simple Purple Martin gourd rack stands over a small Appalachian farm and orchard in the Great Smoky Mountains of Tennessee, circa 1935. *E. E. Exline Archives: Great Smoky Mountains National Park*

THE NEST SITE

Martins return to North America between January and May and sometimes into June. Older birds, called "scouts," return first. Martin decoys and prerecorded dawn songs may help attract martins to nest boxes or gourds. During the first three weeks of nesting, conduct weekly nest checks for missing birds, eggs, signs of predators, and pests like mites. Offer supplemental foods like meals worms and crickets during cold snaps. Clean out and repair gourds and houses in fall. Block entry holes until the martins return in spring; otherwise, sparrows and starlings may claim the territory.

NESTING: As colonial nesters, Purple Martins like living in large groups. Martin houses have multiple compartments; each compartment houses one mated couple and their chicks. The Purple Martin Conservation Association suggests that compartments measuring seven inches by twelve inches and five to seven inches high, may offer better protection against predators and weather than smaller, old-style housing. Females build a nest far back in the room or bowl of the gourd. Both sexes gather nesting

BEHIND THE DESIGN

Ron Seekamp, a retired project engineer and tool designer, built his first martin house from scrap lumber. Over the years, his design evolved as he learned more about martin needs and his own. He discovered advantages to providing "smaller houses with fewer but larger rooms," which had not been the norm. Larger rooms meant a greater chance of 100 percent martin occupancy. And smaller houses were easier to raise and lower. Seekamp, a member of the Minnesota Purple Martin Working Group, was named the Purple Martin Conservation Association's 1999 Landlord of the Year. His martin house plans, meant for moderately experienced woodworkers, are available through the Purple Martin Conservation Association's Martin Market Place, shop.purplemartin.com.

A female Purple Martin arrives in Arroyo City, Texas, in early April 2008. She has likely just made the long journey from South America to return to her summer home. *Ashok Khosla*

A male and female Purple Martin sit on a tiny porch outside their Minnesota condo. A female (at right) flies in with nesting materials. Smaller martin houses with bigger rooms, like this one, may offer advantages over larger martin houses. *Ron Seekamp*

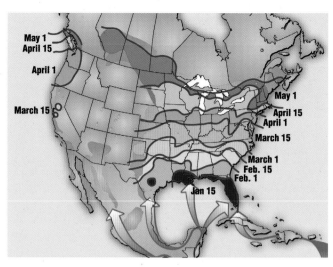

Come spring, Purple Martins arrive in waves from their South American wintering grounds. This chart shows average arrival dates. *Courtesy of the Purple Martin Conservation Society*

materials, including dried grasses, pine needles, leaves, twigs, mud, and fresh green leaves. The leaves, used to cover eggs when parents go out to feed, may keep the eggs humidified.

- **EGGS:** Three to eight pure white eggs.
- **EGG-LAYING:** One per day, usually in the morning.
- **INCUBATION:** Fifteen to eighteen days. Female incubates; both parents feed young.
- **DAYS TO FLEDGE:** Twenty-six to thirty-one days after hatching.

PLACING THE MARTIN HOUSE OR NESTING GOURDS: To ensure a clear flight path, erect housing in the center of the most open spot available, at least sixty to one hundred feet away from human dwellings and away from trees taller than the house. Keep areas under martin homes clear of bushes, shrubs, and vines. Boat docks are good locations for martin houses and gourd racks.

- **NESTING MATERIALS:** Offer dried pine needles and short pieces of wheat straw on raised platforms near the nest for birds to pick and choose from. Place one to two inches of nesting material in each compartment at the start of the season.
- **MOUNTING:** Install metal or wooden poles at least forty feet from overhanging trees or buildings. Make sure housing is easy to raise and lower for frequent nest checks; pulleys and winches are often used. Thwart climbing predators with pole guards and avian predators like crows, hawks, and owls with gourd or martin house "owl guards." Details available at purplemartin.org.
- **HEIGHT:** Place housing at least ten to twenty feet high.

THIS RACK IS MADE FROM
1×4 CYPRESS WOOD, A
TREATED WOOD ALTERNATIVE.

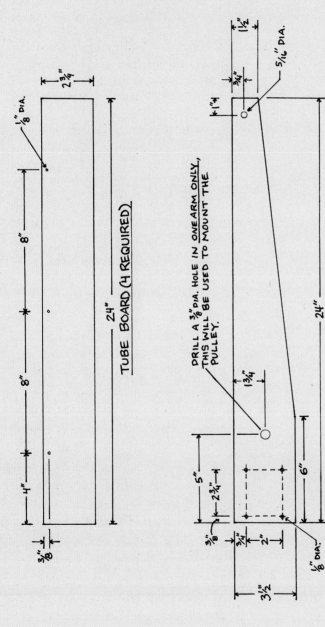

TUBE BOARD (4 REQUIRED)

ARM, (8 REQUIRED)

DRILL A 3/8" DIA. HOLE IN ONE ARM ONLY,
THIS WILL BE USED TO MOUNT THE
PULLEY.

CHUCK'S SIMPLE PURPLE MARTIN RACK
DESIGN BY: CHUCK ABARE
DRAWN BY: CHRIS WILLETT
BOARD CUTS, NOT TO SCALE

PURPLE MARTIN WOODEN GOURD RACK

DESIGNED BY CHUCK ABARE

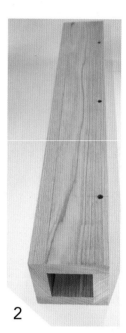

1 Cut the 4" wide board for the four-piece tube slide. Each is 2¾" wide and 24" long. Make initial cuts in the 8" wide board for eight arms.

2 Assemble tube slide. It should fit over a 1½"-diameter galvanized steel pipe with ⅛" to spare, making room for a double-pulley system. Or the tube can be affixed directly onto the pipe.

MATERIALS

- One 1"x4"x8' cypress (used here) or cedar board
- One 1"x8"x8' cypress (used here) or cedar board
- About fifty 2" or 2½" exterior deck screws

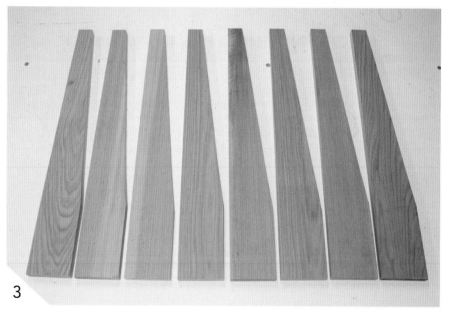

3 Use a table or a circular saw to cut the arms at an angle, "thinning" each of them as per dimensions. One gourd will be attached to the end of each arm.

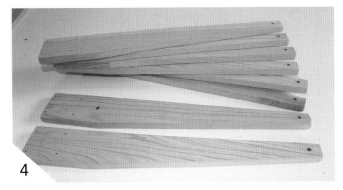

4

Make ⁵⁄₁₆" holes at end of arms. Wire goes through these to hang the gourds. If using pulley system, drill a ³⁄₈" hole in one of the arms. Predrill all deck screw holes.

5

Use some sand paper to take any sharp edges off the arms. (Optional: Round the top edge of each arm with a router. This helps shed water and looks nicer.)

6

Finally, attach the arms to the slide. Look at the photos to visualize the assembly. Stand the tube on end on the workbench, and, taking one arm, screw it to the bottom of the tube, as shown in photos.

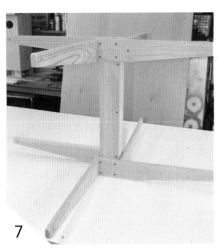

7

Turn the tube 90 degrees and add the second arm. Repeat with the other arms. Keep the arms level. If staining, do it now.

8

Use either plastic gourds or natural gourds that have been pre-dried, hollowed, and cleaned out. To prepare natural gourds, measure and cut two holes: one for the entrance and one for cleaning access.

9

Drill a small hole near the top, through both sides, for the hanging wire. Use caulk to secure the cleaning-hole cover in place. Paint the gourd white—this helps keep the interior cooler by reflecting light.

10

Using natural or plastic gourds, or both, attach the gourds to the rack by stringing wire through the holes at the ends of the rack arms. For easy removal and maintenance, place pole into suitable ground socket, pre-set in concrete. Now just wait for the joyful songs and graceful flight of Purple Martins.

CHAPTER 4

BIRDS OUTSIDE OF BOXES

Not all birds nest inside tree cavities or nest boxes. Some build nests on the boughs and limbs of trees, in the forks of trees, or in the branches of shrubs. Still other birds create homes within natural rock crevices and under rocky overhangs. These days, such places can be scarce.

The following pages will introduce you to some birds that live "outside the box"—those that, when faced with a lack of nesting sites, might choose instead to use either intentionally or unintentionally placed human structures. These might be sheltered places under building eaves, underneath bridges near bodies of water, or even on top of power line distribution poles out in the open. Many of these birds welcome artificial structures designed and built with them in mind; some now nest almost exclusively on such structures.

Small, easily constructed nesting shelves or platforms appeal to American Robins, Barn Swallows, and phoebes. House Finches—a well-named bird—are known to build nests in house gutters and even decorative door wreaths, much to the surprise of the human residents. They can be encouraged to nest on shelves too. Mourning Doves, with their haunting song, can be enticed to nest in specially made hardware cloth cones in backyard trees.

Higher up on the complexity scale are the large nesting platforms that Great Blue Herons and Ospreys need to raise families. People working together can also create artificial chimneys for Chimney Swifts, and artificial loon islands, or rafts, to provide safe havens for Common Loons. Burrowing Owls can be helped by the installation of artificial underground nesting burrows.

Human-provided nesting platforms are credited with helping the recovery of Bald Eagles and Ospreys in the last half of the twentieth century; they have proven to be a successful wildlife management conservation tool. Supplemental nesting sites can make a real and positive difference today, too, especially where natural structures are scarce.

More important, no matter how wonderful the nesting structure is, birds will only nest and successfully breed there if they can find sufficient food, water, and cover nearby. Maintaining healthy ecosystems for birds is key to their preservation.

Pictured here, Osprey juveniles Sky and Sibley test their wings upon the artificial nest platform constructed for them, just prior to fledging in August 2012. Watch nesting Ospreys and Atlantic Puffins— there's even a Puffin Burrow Cam—plus more birds on Audubon's website: projectpuffin. audubon.org/ audubon-live-cams. *Derrick Z. Jackson*

TREE PRUNING FOR NESTS

Trees are not ornaments; they are living organisms and will naturally become a host for other living things. —*Guide to Bird-Friendly Tree and Shrub Trimming*, (c) 2009, Los Angeles Audubon Society

When spring arrives, many people give their property extra care. Often that includes pruning and trimming trees; however, a better time to trim trees and shrubs is during fall and winter, when many trees are dormant.

Spring and summer pruning can spread diseases from tree to tree. In addition, the warmer months are when trees and shrubs are most essential to breeding animals, including birds. As the Los Angeles Audubon Society points out, "Nests may be found at every level of the tree, from the crown to the understory; they may be near the crotch, between branch and trunk, or out toward the end of a branch."

Many species, including wrens, juncos, and finches, build their nests in shrubby thickets near the ground or in shrubs and bushes. American Robins build mud and grass nests in the forks of trees. Orioles and vireos suspend their nests from branches. Woodpeckers hammer out nest cavities in trees that bluebirds, swallows, and other cavity-nesting birds may later use. Great Blue Herons build loose stick nests in the treetops. Hummingbirds and gnatcatchers weave their camouflaged nests onto tree branches.

During annual spring bird walks through local parks and campuses, members of the Los Angeles Audubon Society noticed groundskeepers pruning and trimming shrubs and trees where birds were nesting, or could potentially nest. They saw a need to educate public works departments, land developers, and the general public about the unintentional harm that cutting woody plants can inflict on birds during nesting season. So, in 2009, group members wrote *Guide to Bird-Friendly Tree and Shrub Trimming*. The free guide is available at losangelesaudubon.org.

Members also speak to garden clubs and other groups, encouraging people to view shrubs and trees—including those in their own backyards—as

Vireos use cobwebs to attach their hanging nests to forked twigs on low trees and shrubs. Such forks can be created simply with a pair of pruning shears. *Mark Musselman*

homes for birds and to manage their land to benefit nesting birds.

Waiting until fall to prune shrubs and trees and leaving dead or rotting trees standing—unless they are a threat to people or property—creates a multitude of bird homes, yet requires nothing in terms of time, money, hammers, or nails. It is an easy and natural way to help birds.

Yet another way to help nesting warblers, vireos, thrushes, finches, and sparrows is to prune your trees with birds in mind. Pruning can help create tree forks that will best support their nests. Where three or more branches arise from one location, snip off branches growing vertically rather than horizontally, so that the tree fork lies in a flat plane, creating a natural nest platform. Also, by snipping branches within a fork that are growing too close to one another, you can create a V shape that will allow a nest to hang in between. Birds are selective in choosing branch arrangements that support their nests. With a pair of pruners and a few minutes, you can encourage them to choose nesting branches in your yard.

Mourning Dove   *Zenaida macroura*

A young Mourning Dove rests on a South Carolina deck.
Mark Musselman

Breeding
Year-round
Nonbreeding

The mournful-sounding, fast-flying Mourning Dove is found in every state, from Alaska to Mexico. These birds live in small flocks and begin nesting in early spring, sometimes before the snow has melted. It is estimated that more than twenty million Mourning Doves are shot during hunting season each year, and as ground foragers, they can get lead poisoning from eating fallen lead shot. Despite this, Mourning Dove populations are stable or increasing in most areas.

FIELD MARKS: These foot-long, gray-brown birds have an eighteen-inch wingspan, buffy belly, pale blue ring surrounding dark eyes, plump body, small head, and black spots on the back. In flight, look for gray underwings and a long, pointed tail with large white spots.

VOICE: The doves are named for their distinctively mournful call—a soft, drawn-out *coah, coo, coo, coo.*

FEEDING: Mourning doves feed almost exclusively on the ground, on small weed seeds and grains, providing economic benefits to farmers by controlling weed populations. These birds also visit platform feeders for cracked corn, sunflower seeds, and especially millet.

THE NEST SITE
HELP THROUGHOUT THE SEASONS: Plant conifers or shrubs for nesting and offer special artificial nesting cones or baskets attached to the forks of trees. Provide platform

One of the most abundant and widely hunted birds in the United States, Mourning Doves are sometimes compared to the now-extinct Passenger Pigeon, thought to have numbered in the billions in the mid-1800s. DNA studies show these birds were not closely related, but the story of the once-plentiful Passenger Pigeon flocks provides a cautionary tale. *Linda Cortelyou*

seed feeders or scatter seeds on the ground. Keeping cats indoors helps protect Mourning Doves and other vulnerable ground-feeding birds from predation.

NESTING: Mourning doves frequent open areas, including backyards, fields, deserts, and open forests, as well as human structures like rain gutters and windowsills. Their loose stick-and-pine needle nests are often built in the forks of conifer trees, or in shrubs, or even on the ground. The male gathers materials while the female weaves the nest. These birds are prolific, often raising more than three small broods each season.

- **EGGS:** Two unmarked white eggs.
- **EGG-LAYING:** About one and a half days apart.
- **INCUBATION:** Fourteen to fifteen days. Both parents incubate (males by day, females by night) and feed chicks.
- **DAYS TO FLEDGE:** Twelve to fourteen days.

PLACEMENT: Secure nesting cones or baskets in forked conifer branches with wire at a height of five to twenty-five feet.

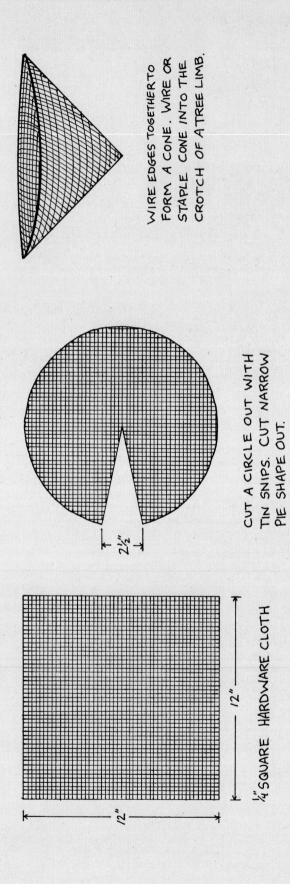

WIRE EDGES TOGETHER TO FORM A CONE. WIRE OR STAPLE CONE INTO THE CROTCH OF A TREE LIMB.

CUT A CIRCLE OUT WITH TIN SNIPS. CUT NARROW PIE SHAPE OUT.

2½"

12"

12"

¼" SQUARE HARDWARE CLOTH

MOURNING DOVE NEST BASKET
DESIGN: NORTHERN PRAIRIE WILDLIFE RESEARCH CENTER (USGS)
DRAWN BY: CHRIS WILLETT
(NOT TO SCALE)

MOURNING DOVE NEST BASKET

MATERIALS

- One 12"x12" square of galvanized metal hardware cloth, with ¼" or ⅜" mesh
- Galvanized wire, approximately 16"

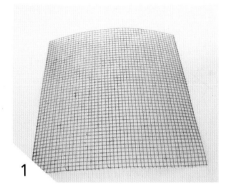

1

With a pair of tin snips cut a 12x12" piece of galvanized hardware cloth.

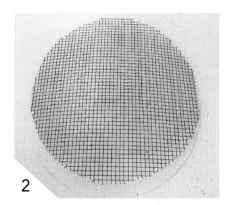

2

Cut a 12" diameter circle out of the piece. Be sure to trim off any sharp protruding wires.

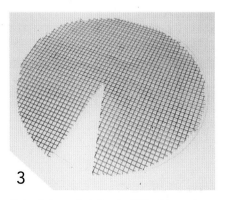

3

Cut a "piece of pie" out: 2½" wide on the "crust side."

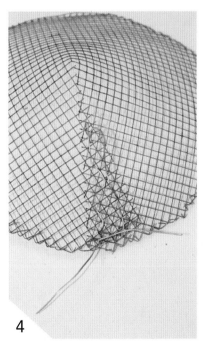

4

Fold the circle to make a cone, and "sew" it together with a wire at the seam.

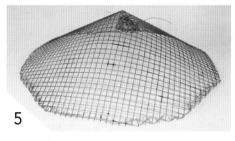

5

Fold the top of the cone over so no sharp edges face the nest basket area. Hang in an appropriate location in the crotch of a conifer tree branch by wiring it to the branch in several places.

SWALLOWS

Barn Swallow

Hirundo rustica

Male and female Barn Swallows differ only slightly in appearance. The female's tail is shorter than the male's; she is also paler and less glossy. It's unclear whether this bird is a male or female.
Ashok Khosla

Breeding

Breeding & wintering

Wintering

Barn Swallows soar over open country with effortless grace in pursuit of flying insects. Since they have long used human structures as nest sites, populations of this species expanded as settlers spread across North America. Barn Swallows have one of the longest land bird migrations—up to 7,000 miles from Alaska to Argentina.

RANGE: The Barn Swallow's huge range includes Asia, Europe, Africa, and the Americas.

FIELD MARKS: These swallows are about seven inches long, blue-black above, and cinnamon or orange below, with a dark throat, long, slender, pointed wings spanning fifteen inches and a long, deeply forked, white spotted tail. Males have longer tail feathers and darker orange underparts than females.

VOICE: Call is a soft *witt* or *witt-witt*. Song is a long musical warble, often ending in *su-seer*.

FEEDING: Barn Swallows feed on insects caught in flight; they can eat, drink, and bathe on the wing. They may also fly behind tractors, catching displaced grasshoppers and crickets.

Barn Swallows collect mud pellets, which they'll use to build a nest.
Vishnevskly Vasily

THE NEST SITE

HELP THROUGHOUT THE SEASONS: Barn Swallows live in close association with humans and are often welcomed for their insect-eating habits. To attract them to your property, install a six-inch-square nesting platform in a garage or shed with an open door or window. Barn Swallows prefer unpainted, rough-cut wood, as their mud nests will not adhere well to smooth surfaces. Keep a small area in your yard muddy or offer a tray of mud near the building entrance near the swallows' nest. This will save the birds the time-consuming chore of traveling

Barn Swallows are superb aerialists, making quick turns and dives. In flight the bird may spread its distinctive "swallow tail," revealing showy white dots. *Ashok Khosla*

to a distant stream for each beakful of mud. If you do not have an established breeding site, play prerecorded Barn Swallow songs to encourage colonization.

NESTING: Although they once nested in caves, cliffs, and rock crevices, these colonial nesters now use the shelter of barns, sheds, porches, boat docks, and even the undersides of Osprey nests. Nests are usually built on a vertical surface just below a ceiling, allowing little overhead space. The cup nest is made of mud mixed with fine grass, plastered to a surface, and lined with horsehair and feathers.

- **EGGS:** May be two to seven, usually four to five white eggs speckled with brown.
- **EGG-LAYING:** One per morning.
- **INCUBATION:** Thirteen to seventeen days. Both parents incubate and feed young.
- **DAYS TO FLEDGE:** Eighteen to twenty-three days.

PLACEMENT: Install L-shaped nesting shelves or platforms under an overhead roof. Ideal nearby habitats include open pastures, farm fields, and meadows with abundant flying insects, preferably near water.

L-SHAPED PLATFORM FOR BARN SWALLOWS

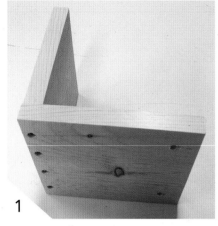

1

Cut a 1x6x12¾" pine, cedar, or cypress board according to the drawing. Make two keyhole attachments on top of back piece. Predrill four holes at the bottom, and attach the floor with four 1½" exterior screws.

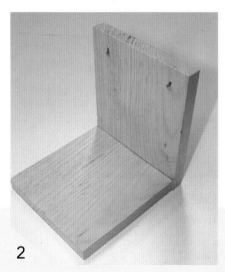

2

Hang appropriately.

MATERIALS

- One 1x6x12¾" cedar, cypress, or pine board
- Four 2" exterior grade deck screws

L- SHAPED PLATFORM
FOR BARN SWALLOWS

PROTECTED AREAS
ADAPTED FROM: STEVE KRESS
DRAWN BY: CHRIS WILLETT

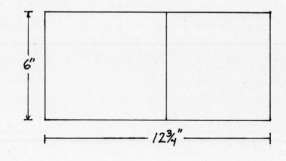

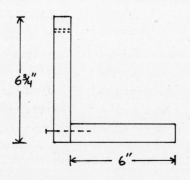

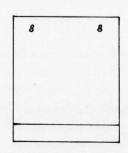

American Robin

Turdus migratorius

Robins are often visible when foraging on the ground, but catch most of their insect prey on tree foliage or in the air. *Ashok Khosla*

- Breeding
- Breeding & wintering
- Wintering

American Robins are ubiquitous across North America—in parks, backyards, golf courses, fields, and forests. Although most are resident or short-distance migrants, birds that breed farther north often fly south in fall. Come winter, these members of the thrush family may form flocks of hundreds and beyond, gathering in trees to roost and feed. In summer, when foraging on lawns, their vulnerability to pesticide poisoning makes robins important pollution indicators.

RANGE: Widespread throughout the United States and Canada.

FIELD MARKS: This midsized bird, the largest of the North American thrushes, is about ten inches long, with a seventeen-inch wingspan, dark gray back, brick-red breast, and dark head, nape, and tail. The female is paler overall. In flight, look for a white patch on the belly and under the tail, and smooth, flicking wing beats.

VOICE: Song is a clear, musical caroling with short rising and falling phrases, often the first bird song heard on spring mornings. Calls include *tyeep* and *tut-tut-tut*.

FEEDING: Robins eat different foods in different seasons. In autumn and winter, they eat mostly fruits and berries. Fruit supplies are also important in early spring, when snow cover prevents ground feeding. When days grow warm in spring and summer, they switch to soft invertebrates like earthworms. Although they appear to be listening, the robins' habit of cocking their heads to one side enables them to better see the earthworms. It is common to see robins on the ground after a rain or water sprinkling. That's when the worms come out and make easy pickings for the birds.

THE NEST SITE

HELP THROUGHOUT THE SEASONS: Plant cherries for summer food; black gum, and flowering dogwood for fall food; and sumac, crabapple, and hawthorn trees for good winter sustenance. Robins can be attracted to feeders with mealworms. Offer birdbaths; these birds seem to enjoy a good splash.

NESTING: Robins require mature trees for nesting and singing. Early spring nests are typically built in protected conifers; later nests are built in deciduous trees. Others nest in unintended human structures, including rain gutters and eaves, as well as intentional nesting structures such as shelves. Females build nests from grass, twigs, paper, feathers, rootlets, and moss, then reinforce it with mud and line it with fine dry grass. Robins are highly territorial when nesting. They may produce three broods per year.

- **EGGS:** Three to five sky-blue or blue-green eggs.
- **EGG-LAYING:** One per day.
- **INCUBATION:** Twelve to fourteen days. Female incubates; both parents feed.
- **DAYS TO FLEDGE:** Thirteen to fifteen days.

PLACEMENT: Place nesting shelves under the eaves of porches and barns.

Like the bluebird—a fellow member of the thrush family—the robin's breast is speckled when young. *Ashok Khosla*

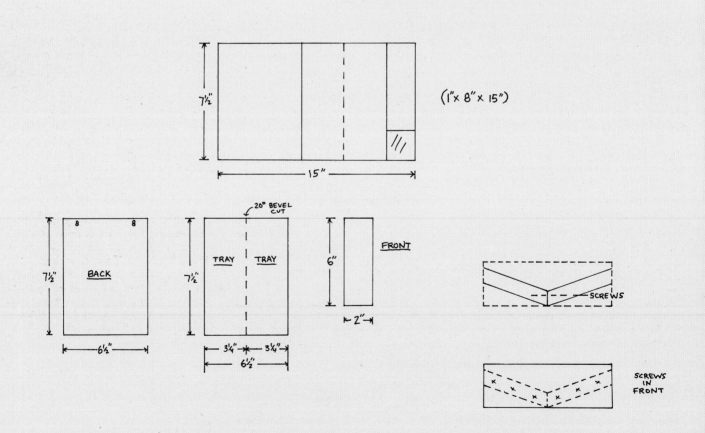

V-SHAPED SHELF FOR AMERICAN ROBINS, HOUSE FINCHES, AND PHOEBES
PROTECTED AREAS
ADAPTED FROM: KRESS (1985)
DRAWN BY: CHRIS WILLETT

V-SHAPED SHELF FOR ROBINS, PHOEBES, AND HOUSE FINCHES

MATERIALS

- One 1x8x15" cedar, cypress, or pine board
- Eight to ten 2" exterior grade deck screws

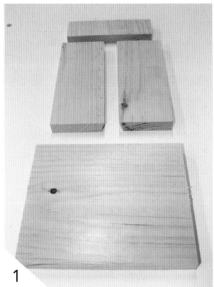

1

Start with a 1x8x15" pine, cedar, or cypress board. Cut to the specifications on the drawing. Make two keyhole attachment points at the top of the back piece.

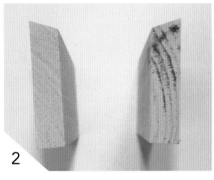

2

Cut a 20-degree angle along the 8"-long side of one edge of each of the floor pieces.

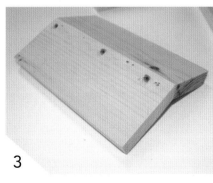

3

Attach together with four 1¼" exterior-grade screws. Predrill to avoid splitting the wood (see drawing).

4

Attach the 2x6" reinforcement piece to the front of the tray with several screws. Drill three or four ¼" weep holes in the bottom of the tray. Set the tray down on the back and trace the shape; this can then be predrilled for screw placement. Doing this will help you with accuracy, as the tray is screwed in from the back. Attach the tray to the back piece, approximately 1" up from bottom.

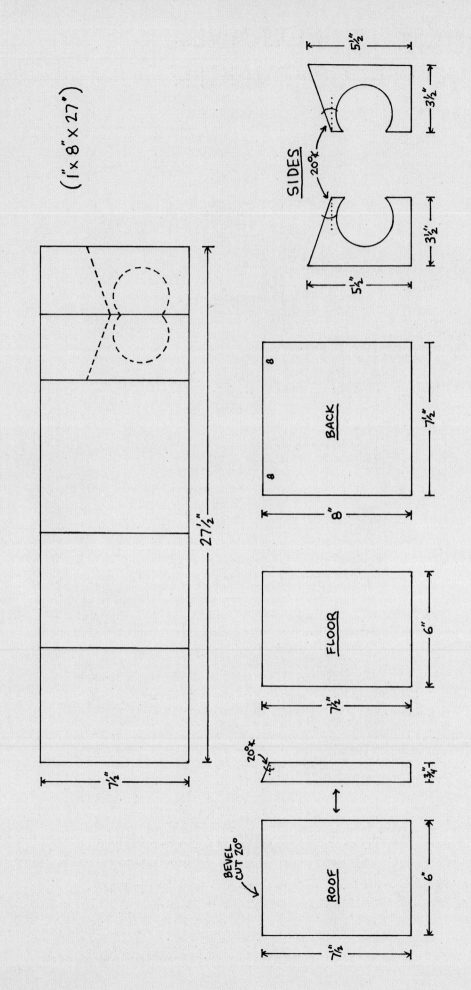

(1" × 8" × 27")

27½"

7½"

BEVEL CUT 20°

ROOF

7½"

6"

20°

1¾"

FLOOR

7½"

6"

BACK

8"

8

8

7½"

SIDES

20°

5½"

3½"

5½"

3½"

COVERED SHELF FOR AMERICAN ROBINS, HOUSE FINCHES, AND PHOEBES

SEMI-EXPOSED AREAS

ADAPTED FROM: KRESS (1985)
DRAWN BY: CHRIS WILLETT

COVERED SHELF FOR ROBINS, PHOEBES, AND HOUSE FINCHES

1

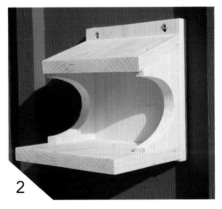

2

Attach the sides to the bottom and back, and then attach the roof to the sides and back. Be sure to predrill to avoid splitting the wood. Make two keyhole hangers in the back piece to attach to a wall or eave area. Hang appropriately.

Start with a 1x8x27" pine, cedar, or cypress board. Cut out pieces according to the drawing. Cut 20-degree angles at the top of the two sides and on one edge of the roof piece, which attaches to the back (see drawing). Cut a half circle out of the side pieces (note the drawing) using a jigsaw. Attach the floor to the back piece; be sure to predrill four locations evenly, so that the screws' points will not be exposed in circle cutouts. Attach with 1¼" exterior screws. Be sure to recess approximately ¼" from the bottom.

MATERIALS

- One 1x8x27" cedar, cypress, or pine board
- Ten to twelve 2" exterior grade deck screws

House Finch

Carpodacus mexicanus

To discover a House Finch nest near your home, try and follow the bird as it flies away from your feeders. It just might be heading back to the nest. *Mark Musselman*

Year-round

Originally a bird of southwestern deserts and grasslands, House Finches were introduced to the eastern United States in 1939. When threatened with prosecution under the Migratory Bird Treaty Act of 1918, pet store vendors in Long Island, New York, released illegal stocks of caged California-caught "Hollywood Finches." The first eastern House Finch nest was found in Babylon, New York, in 1944. A half-century later, the western and eastern populations met. Soon after, the birds' expansion was slowed by disease: West Nile virus, avian pox, and avian conjunctivitis (a potentially fatal, bacteria-caused eye disease). Despite these challenges, House Finches are one of the most commonly seen feeder birds.

RANGE: Widespread across the continental United States and on all of the Hawaiian Islands.

FIELD MARKS: This five-and-a-half-inch-long bird has a slightly notched tail, which looks long in comparison to its short, rounded wings. Males have a bright red to orange or yellowish head, neck, and breast, a brownish back, and streaked flanks. Males with a more diverse diet tend to be more colorful. Females, which are a dull grayish-brown and lack head stripes, prefer the more colorful males.

VOICE: Bright, loose, rapid, cheery warble, frequently ending in a nasal *che-urrr*. Males sing loud, continuous courtship songs.

FEEDING: Although House Finches have a notorious appetite for sunflower seeds, their principal foods are weed seeds like thistle and dandelion. They also eat pigment-rich fruits and berries, from which males derive their color. In Hawaii, they are known as the "papaya bird" because of their penchant for that fruit. Unlike most chicks, House Finch nestlings are fed exclusively plant foods.

House Finches are creative when it comes to nesting sites. The center of this hanging fern contains a cup nest filled with newly hatched House Finches (below). *Mark Musselman*

A hanging-fern home seems to suit these down-covered nestlings. House Finch pairs seek nest sites under covered areas. *Mark Musselman*

THE NEST SITE

HELP THROUGHOUT THE SEASONS: As their name implies, House Finches benefit from their association with people and their houses. They nest behind gutters, light fixtures, or other building protrusions, as well as in ivy growing on buildings, and in suitable objects around houses, including hanging plant pots, small baskets, and evergreen wreaths. Provide fresh water in birdbaths, and stock feeders with black oil sunflower seeds. Keep feeders and birdbaths clean to help prevent diseases from spreading.

NESTING: Male courtship displays in early spring include a back-and-forth swaying close to the female. The females build grass nests around houses, porches, barns, or garages, often incorporating hair, string, cotton, and wool. Brown-headed Cowbirds often lay eggs in House Finch nests, but the finches' vegetarian diet may not be adequate for cowbird young.

- **EGGS:** Four to five pale gray-green eggs spotted with purple, brown, and black.
- **EGG-LAYING:** One egg per day.
- **INCUBATION:** Twelve to fourteen days. Female incubates; both parents feed.
- **DAYS TO FLEDGE:** Twelve to nineteen days.

PLACEMENT: House Finches seek nesting sites with a roof overhead. A hanging plant, wreath, or easy-to-build nesting platform offers a ready-made home for a House Finch family. Place such objects away from doors and other high-traffic areas.

THE BUILD

House Finches will nest on a platform: see pages 130–132 for plans.

Eastern Phoebe

Sayornis phoebe

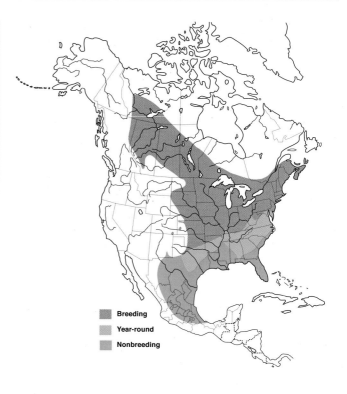

Eastern Phoebes were likely the first birds ever banded in North America. In 1804, when little was known about bird migration, John James Audubon tied silver threads around the legs of Eastern Phoebe nestlings near his Pennsylvania home. The following spring, a phoebe with a silver leg "bracelet" returned to the same yard from where it had hatched. *Ashok Khosla*

- Breeding
- Year-round
- Nonbreeding

Say's Phoebe

Sayornis saya

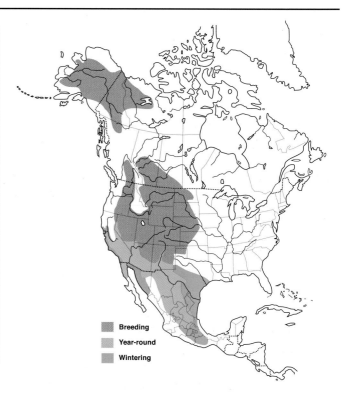

Say's Phoebes eat mainly insects year-round. *Ashok Khosla*

- Breeding
- Year-round
- Wintering

This Eastern Phoebe has chosen an exposed perch from which to dart out for insect prey. Phoebes will often return to the same hunting spot. Another characteristic trait of phoebes is flicking the tail and wings in a nervous, twitchy manner. *Ashok Khosla*

Just like an Eastern Phoebe, this Say's Phoebe will "flycatch" from the perch and snatch insects in mid-air. *Ashok Khosla*

Eastern Phoebes once nested along stream-bank cliffs and overhangs, but these adaptable birds now usually nest on porches, under house eaves and bridges, on barns and sheds, and even in active doorways. Say's Phoebes have also benefited from nesting in and around human-made structures and have a wide breeding range. Because nesting sites are plentiful, phoebe populations are stable in most areas.

RANGE: Eastern Phoebes breed throughout eastern North America up into some western Canadian provinces and generally winter in the southeastern United States or Mexico. Say's Phoebes are found in the West, from Alaska to Mexico, and are short to medium-distance migrants.

FIELD MARKS: Eastern Phoebes are gray-brown and about seven inches long, with a ten-and-a-half-inch wing-span. While perched in silhouette, they can be identified by their upright posture and tail-wagging behavior. Say's Phoebe is larger but more slender, with brownish-gray upper parts and a buffy orange belly.

VOICE: The Eastern Phoebe sings its two-part name, a burry, well-enunciated *fee-bee*. Its call is a sharp peep or chip. A common Say's Phoebe song is *phee-ur*.

FEEDING: Phoebes use their wide, flat bills for catching flying insects or gleaning insects from foliage, often making short flights from a perch to capture beetles, wasps, and bees. Eastern Phoebes eat berries and seeds in winter. Say's Phoebes are more insectivorous, eating mostly insects year-round.

THE NEST SITE
HELP THROUGHOUT THE SEASONS: Phoebes like nesting in wooded yards and in human-made structures, wherever they might find a sheltered ledge. Even in northern areas, Eastern Phoebes can start building nests in late March, while Say's Phoebes in Alaska might not complete their nests until late May. Both depend on shrubs for gleaning insects and small trees for perches. Providing abundant understory plants, including berry and insect-attracting plants, improves habitat for these birds.

NESTING: Eastern Phoebes may renovate previously used phoebe or Barn Swallow nests. Their substantial mud-and-grass nests are covered with moss, and the circular nest cup is lined with hair and fine grasses. Phoebe nests are often parasitized by Brown-headed Cowbirds. Say's Phoebes rarely use mud to construct nests.
- EGGS: Usually four to five white eggs with spots. Two or three broods per year.
- EGG-LAYING: One per day, usually in the morning
- INCUBATION: Sixteen days. Female incubates; both parents feed chicks.
- DAYS TO FLEDGE: Fifteen to sixteen days.

PLACEMENT: A six-by-six-inch wooden shelf can serve as a nesting platform, especially if secured under an eave or overhang. Say's Phoebes are less likely to nest on artificial shelves.

THE BUILD
These phoebes will nest on a platform: see pages 130–132 for plans.

Burrowing Owl   *Athene cunicularia*

Burrowing Owls outside their burrow at southern California's Salton Sea National Wildlife Refuge. *Ashok Khosla*

Breeding

Year-round

Nonbreeding

A Burrowing Owl perched on a cattle ranch fence near Jeremoabao, Brazil. The owls are widespread throughout Mexico and Central and South America. *Ashok Khosla*

As the name suggests, Burrowing Owls nest underground, typically in burrows excavated by other animals. These diminutive owls are endangered in Canada, threatened in Mexico, and declining in many areas, including Florida and the western United States—primarily due to prairie dog extermination programs, habitat loss, and car collisions, as well as outdoor cats and unleashed dogs. Populations are increasing in deforested areas of the Amazon, however.

RANGE: Found in grasslands and arid regions of western North America, Florida, and the Caribbean.

FIELD MARKS: Burrowing Owls are small for owls—about nine and a half inches long, with a twenty-two-inch wingspan. Their coloration is brown and white with whitish spots on the back and barring on front. They have long legs and short tails. Their eyes are bright yellow. Eyebrows are white and prominent. They lack ear tufts. Males and females are similar in size and appearance.

VOICE: A two-note *coo coooo* song. Also utters a series of rattling, clucking, and chattering calls.

FEEDING: Burrowing Owls hunt at night, using their night vision and hearing as they swoop down or fly up to catch flying insects or chase prey across the ground on foot. Their varied diet includes small insects like beetles and earwigs, large insects, small rodents, birds, amphibians, and reptiles. A University of Florida study suggests that Burrowing Owls may also bait their burrows with dung to attract beetles.

A cinder-block entrance to a Burrowing Owl nest helps stabilize the artificial burrow below and protects against predators. Coyotes in particular may dig up burrows in search of prey; cinder blocks make it harder for them to do that. *Scott and Heather Artis*

THE NEST SITE

HELP THROUGHOUT THE SEASONS: Burrowing Owls often inhabit human landscapes, such as airports, fields, and golf courses. They readily use artificial nest sites, whether in unintentionally buried pieces of pipe or specially designed plastic and wooden burrows with easy access to the surface; the latter were first tested in California in the 1970s. Clean and repair artificial burrows before nesting begins. Heaping a small amount of soil around the tunnel entrance may help attract owls. On ranches, burrows should be strong enough to withstand the weight of livestock that might stand on nesting sites.

In Florida and California, some Burrowing Owls place "treasures" in front of their entrance holes. At this Burrowing Owl entrance hole, many pieces of bark, as well as a corncob, paper, and a shell have been collected. *Scott and Heather Artis*

Because Burrowing Owls sometimes have a primary burrow and a satellite burrow—adult male owls will often use the satellite burrow to store food for chicks—install artificial burrows in pairs where space permits.

NESTING: Nesting burrows are usually pre-excavated by animals such as ground squirrels, prairie dogs, armadillos, or tortoises. Owls can excavate too, by kicking back soil with their feet and digging with their beaks. Burrows are often reused for several consecutive years. Natural burrows can be several convoluted yards long. Owl "treasures" like bark, uneaten frogs, cigarette butts, tin foil, paper, and plastic have been found at the entrance holes of burrows in California and Florida.

- **EGGS:** Four to twelve, usually nine, white round eggs.
- **EGG-LAYING:** Every one or two days.
- **INCUBATION:** Three to four weeks. Female incubates; both parents feed chicks.
- **DAYS TO FLEDGE:** Four weeks; usually only half the chicks survive.

PLACEMENT: Burrowing Owls are at home in pastures, cemeteries, agricultural fields, and deserts; however, any open, dry area with low vegetation may suffice. Artificial burrows should be located in high, well-drained areas to avoid flooding.

- **MOUNTING:** Place artificial burrows several feet underground, with entry holes at ground level.

SAVING SAN FRANCISCO BAY'S BURROWING OWLS

In California, Santa Clara Valley Audubon Society volunteers are working with the city of Mountain View to enhance and manage a local urban park to benefit Burrowing Owls. Shoreline Park is a closed landfill on the San Francisco Bay's south side. The owls there face a shortage of prey and nesting sites. So, native perennial plants are routinely planted to attract the insects and rodents that the owls feed on. An insect called the earwig is the number-one prey item, followed by beetles, grasshoppers, and then "higher quality" food, including pocket gophers, mice, and California voles.

Ground squirrels are welcome at the park, since they excavate natural burrows later used by the owls. Artificial nesting burrows are installed too. Six-inch-diameter plastic corrugated pipes, angled at forty-five degrees for an entryway, work best in Shoreline Park, says Mountain View biologist and Burrowing Owl specialist Phil Higgins. He opens the pipes at the bottom by cutting out two-inch pieces. "The birds seem to like having soil under their feet while going in and out of their home," he says. That "home" is a small plastic open-ended box placed about four feet underground and connected to the entryway.

This artificial burrow, installed by birder and photographer Steve Simmons, uses a strong plywood box with a handled lid for easy access. It is placed two feet underground and attached to an eight-foot-long corrugated plastic pipe, which is connected to a smaller box at the entry. Backhoes are first used to dig out the soil. *Steve Simmons*

The steel pipe affixed to this removable nest box lid allows the photographer to drop a camera into the burrow. *Steve Simmons*

THE BUILD

Several artificial burrow plans are contained in a guide that can be downloaded from the Burrowing Owl Conservation Network: burrowingowlconservation. org/publications.html.

Users Guide to Installation of Artificial Burrows for Burrowing Owls, David H. Johnson, Donald C. Gillis, Michael A. Gregg, James L. Rebholz, Jeffrey L. Lincer, and James R. Belthoff. Selah, Wash.: Tree Top Inc., August 2010.

A Burrowing Owl nest tunnel plan can be found in *Woodworking for Wildlife*, by Carrol L. Henderson. St. Paul, Minn.: Minnesota Department of Natural Resources, 2009.

LOONS

Common Loon

Gavia immer

Young loons can swim shortly after hatching. They often hitch a ride on a parent's back. At just eight weeks, they are diving to find their own food, including small minnows, leeches, and aquatic insects. They will spend most of their lives on water. *June LeDuc*

Breeding

Wintering

For many, the nocturnal echoing of Common Loon calls across clear lakes is a symbol of the northern woods. Although well adapted to water, loons are awkward on land and typically come ashore only to nest. Regional population declines have occurred, due in part to acid rain, mercury from coal-burning plants, ocean oil spills, heavily developed shorelines, and the birds' susceptibility to flooding and human disturbance. Dogs, motorboats, canoes, and kayaks can all cause loon parents to abandon their nest or young if they get too close. In New England, the ingestion of discarded or lost lead fishing weights kills more loons than any other cause.

RANGE: Common Loons breed throughout Canada and parts of the northern United States. They are considered mid-distance migrants and winter in coastal marine areas.

FIELD MARKS: These large waterbirds have long bodies, short tails, and dagger-like bills. Their legs are set far back on the body, restricting movement on land but helping them swim efficiently. In flight, the feet protrude beyond the tail. Summer adults are distinctive, with a black-and-white checker pattern on the back and wings, and a partial white collar. In winter, they turn gray above and white below.

VOICE: A single loon's haunting wail may be answered by a chorus of other loons, as the birds announce their location. Male loons also produce a signature territorial yodel, which may change if the territory changes.

FEEDING: Made less buoyant by solid bones and propelled by powerful feet, loons submerge silently and pursue fish rapidly, swallowing their prey underwater. In northern lakes, small fish such as perch and sunfish make up most of their diet.

THE NEST SITE

HELP THROUGHOUT THE SEASONS: Because they are so close to water, loon nests are vulnerable to flooding. Wooden or PVC artificial nesting platforms or rafts act as "floating islands" and allow the birds to ride out fluctuations in water levels. These rafts must be properly anchored, checked, and maintained. Common Loons require lakes clean enough to see prey underwater and about a quarter mile of open water as a runway for "takeoff." Lakes with sheltered coves and islands provide refuge from predators during nesting season, typically May to July. Keep garbage far away from nesting sites to help loons avoid egg predators like skunks and raccoons. When stressed at the nest site, loons will put their heads down, a sign that it is time to leave the area.

Loons seek concealed lakeside settings in which to build their well-camouflaged grass nests. The nest at this idyllic Maine pond site took the loon pair about a week to build. Maine Audubon suggests the best way to watch nesting loons is with binoculars from a spot that is a respectful distance from the nest. *June LeDuc*

NESTING: Mated loon pairs build a nest together in late spring, in a quiet, hidden lakeshore area, creating a nest mound camouflaged to look like a clump of dead marsh grass. They then climb atop the mound and shape a nest depression about two feet wide. Nesting pairs often refurbish a previous nest rather than build a new one.

- **EGGS:** Usually two brown eggs with dark splotches. One brood per year.
- **EGG-LAYING:** About two days apart.
- **INCUBATION:** Twenty-six to twenty-nine days
- **DAYS TO FLEDGE:** Chicks are able to swim and ride on parent's back soon after hatching, but can't fly for another six to eight weeks.

PLACEMENT: Place artificial nesting platforms on clear lakes with coves, islands, and abundant small fish.

THE BUILD
ARTIFICIAL NESTING PLATFORMS FOR COMMON LOONS: Maine Audubon's Loon Project offers loon-friendly tips and several artificial nesting platform designs on its website: maineaudubon.org/wildlife-habitat/the-maine-loon-project.

The Vermont Loon Recovery Project offers more information about artificial nesting platforms. To download the booklet *Guidelines for Use of Artificial Nesting Rafts for Common Loons*, go to: vtecostudies.org/loons.

Learn more about loon projects from The Loon Network, at loonnetwork.org.

CREATING LOON-FRIENDLY HABITAT

Since 1983, Audubon's Maine Loon Project has worked to monitor the state's loons. On the third Saturday of every July, "citizen scientists" from all over Maine—nearly a thousand in 2012—rise early in the morning, settle themselves near a lake or pond at 7 a.m., and spend the next half hour counting loons. Their data forms are then compiled to reveal the health of Maine's loon populations. Says project director Susan Gallo, "Volunteers spend countless hours, not just on loon count day but throughout the summer, monitoring how well loon pairs are doing, how many chicks they raise, and the quality of nesting habitat on their lakes."

Adding vegetation (like shrubs) to the cedar rafts provides cover for the loons, especially from boaters and predators. *Emily Sloan*

Cedar logs are used to build loon rafts for the Vermont Loon Recovery Project. Members of the Vermont Youth Conservation Corps notch the cedar logs and fit them together "Lincoln-log style." *Eric Hanson, courtesy of the Vermont Center for Ecostudies*

SWIFTS

Chimney Swift

Chaetura pelagica

The Chimney Swift's dark color, cylindrical body, and short stubby tail have inspired some to dub the birds "flying cigars."
Rebecca Field, Audubon Minnesota

☐ Breeding

Before the development of eastern North America, Chimney Swifts probably nested in hollow trees and caves. After European settlement, they took advantage of chimneys for nesting and roosting and populations grew. More recently, these birds have declined—some populations by half—throughout their range. Possible reasons include deforestation in the birds' Amazonian winter grounds, along with the deterioration and capping of older chimneys, and changes in design that render new chimneys less hospitable. Like many insect-eating long distance migrants, they are also vulnerable to pesticides throughout the year and to migration hazards, including collisions with lighted cell towers.

RANGE: Chimney Swifts breed throughout the eastern United States into southern Canada. By November, they have migrated thousands of miles south to overwinter in South America. A portion of the Chimney Swift's wintering grounds were discovered in 1943 when bands from thirteen swifts banded in North America were recovered in Peru.

FIELD MARKS: Described as "cigars with wings," these cylindrical five-inch-long birds are outstanding aerialists that glide along between bursts of rapid, erratic flight. The name "swift" fits: These birds are built for speed, with long, pointed wings, tiny beaks and feet, and stiff, stubby tails. Except for nesting and evening roosting, they rarely land. Unlike other birds, they cannot perch on wires or branches but are well adapted for clinging to rough vertical surfaces. A similar but smaller Pacific Northwest species is Vaux's Swift. Both birds have inspired conservation efforts.

VOICE: Call is a loud, rapid, ticking or high-pitched twittering. Soft cheeps from nestlings often alert homeowners to the birds' presence in a chimney.

FEEDING: The Chimney Swift's large mouth opens in flight to capture a wide range of flying insects, including flies, beetles, and termites, as it forages over open areas. The birds' fondness for insects makes them beloved by humans.

THE NEST SITE

HELP THROUGHOUT THE SEASONS: Before the Chimney Swifts' early spring arrival, remove chimney caps and close dampers. Clean chimneys of creosote and other debris. Avoid cleaning chimneys or using fireplaces during the birds' nesting season; heat and toxic gases can be fatal. Keep metal chimneys capped at all times. They can trap swifts and other creatures. Conservation efforts focus on building artificial nesting towers as chimney substitutes. Because swifts are often confused with bats, identification is another important part of swift conservation.

TOWERING EFFORTS FOR CHIMNEY SWIFTS

Audubon Minnesota has been working to restore Chimney Swift populations since 2009. The organization's multipronged approach includes building wooden Chimney Swift nesting towers, saving historic old chimneys, and organizing community events such as A Swift Night Out in late summer, when observers watch and count the number of birds funneling back into their homes at night to roost. Ron Windingstad of the Audubon At Home program says retired woodworkers, especially, have stepped up to build towers for Minnesota's Chimney Swifts. "Many have donated considerable skills and shop time, as well as becoming mentors for young people," he says. One of the highlights of his career has been to witness groups of young and old teaching each other about woodworking and birds, as together they craft a hands-on bird conservation project, he says. Of course, another highlight for the entire group is when Chimney Swifts begin to call these towers home.

In Minnesota, more than two hundred Boy Scouts built thirty-seven wooden Chimney Swift towers in just two years. Johnny Her, an Eagle Scout, was awarded a grant to build many of these towers. Here, he attaches a sun-collar top to the eighteen-foot tower while other scouts steady the ladder; still others mix cement to pour into the wooden form at the base. The tower's four steel feet will rest in the concrete foundation, providing stability for the structure. *Ron Windingstad, Audubon Minnesota*

A Chimney Swift flies head first into an artificial nesting tower at the Gulf Coast Bird Observatory in Lake Jackson, Texas. The towers replicate older-style chimneys, which over many years, Chimney Swifts grew used to nesting in. *Michael L. Gray, courtesy of the Gulf Coast Bird Observatory*

NESTING: Chimney Swifts grab twigs from tree branches with their feet while in flight, then transfer them to their mouths. Using their glue-like saliva, the birds then construct a small, cup-like twig nest, and attach it to the nesting structure's inner wall.

- EGGS: Usually four to five white eggs with brown speckles.
- EGG-LAYING: Every other day.
- INCUBATION: Nineteen to twenty-one days.
- DAYS TO FLEDGE: Twenty-eight to thirty days. Chicks stay in the nest longer than most similar-sized birds.

Chimney Swifts are silhouetted in early evening as they swarm around their nighttime roost—an old-style brick chimney. Such structures are disappearing with changing times, but specially designed towers may help take their place.
Jim Williams, Audubon Minnesota

A Chimney Swift rests after being rescued from a sweltering hospital attic in Texas. About a hundred of the birds were brought to the Gulf Coast Bird Observatory, where they scooped up fresh water from nearby wetlands before circling up high and flying away. *Michael L. Gray, courtesy of the Gulf Coast Bird Observatory*

This free-standing 12-foot-tall Chimney Swift tower with a kiosk below was built at Minnesota's Orono Schools Nature Center as one Boy Scout's project.
Ron Windingstad, Audubon Minnesota

PLACEMENT: Place towers in areas free of vegetation and vines. Space at least ten feet apart where possible.
- MOUNTING: Towers should be secure enough to withstand strong winds.
- HEIGHT: Typically twelve feet high.

THE BUILD

CHIMNEY SWIFT TOWER PLANS: Chimney Swift towers are described as "mini-chimney replicas" that function as both nest sites and nighttime shelters. Despite their twelve-foot height, the average sixteen-by-sixteen-inch base means they also fit well into small backyards. Building a Chimney Swift tower is a good community project. Groups like bird clubs and scout troops often build them in public places such as schools and parks.

Chimney Swift tower woodworking plans can be found in the book *Chimney Swift Towers: New Habitat for America's Mysterious Birds* by Paul D. Kyle and Georgean Z. Kyle (2005). Another book by the Kyles, *Chimney Swifts: America's Mysterious Birds above the Fireplace* (2005), focuses on chimney swift biology and conservation.

For more information, including how-to videos on Chimney Swift tower construction, go to ChimneySwifts.org.

Great Blue Heron

Ardea herodias

The dark stripe above the Great Blue Heron's eye extends into slender black plumes. Heron plumes were prized by hunters during the feather trade era of the late 1800s to early 1900s. *Ashok Khosla*

Breeding
Year-round
Nonbreeding

Great Blue Herons can be identified in flight by their tucked necks and extended legs. *Ashok Khosla*

In the late nineteenth century and early twentieth century, Great Blue Herons were slaughtered for their showy plumes, which were used to adorn women's hats and clothes. Populations were drastically reduced but subsequently recovered following protective legislation. Today, the heron population is again declining, particularly where pesticides, mercury, and other pollutants have contaminated the herons' wetland feeding areas. Great Blue Herons are also vulnerable to habitat loss and human disturbances that disrupt nesting colonies, including vehicle traffic, logging, and motorboats.

RANGE: Widespread throughout most of North America except at high elevations. This partial migrant usually leaves northern areas in winter.

FIELD MARKS: This largest North American heron stands three to four feet tall, with a wingspan of almost six feet. Blue-gray feathers cover most of its body. It has a long, pointed yellow bill, black stripe over the eye, and long legs. In breeding season, shaggy plumes appear on the back and neck. An all-white subspecies resides in southern Florida. In flight, look for an S-shaped neck and legs that extend beyond the tail.

VOICE: Herons produce a harsh croaking or squawking call. They are most vocal during the breeding season.

FEEDING: Great Blue Herons wade slowly through shallow water, typically around dawn and dusk. They strike with lightning speed, quickly plucking up frogs, reptiles, small mammals, insects, and other birds.

A foggy morning at the Almond Marsh Forest Preserve heron rookery in Illinois. The birds are nesting on both natural and artificial "trees." *Allison Frederick, courtesy Lake County Forest Preserves*

THE NEST SITE

HELP THROUGHOUT THE SEASONS: Great Blue Herons aren't typical backyard visitors, but sometimes will visit yards with fishponds. Although these herons nest mainly in trees, they also use human-provided structures such as duck blinds, channel markers, or artificial nest platforms. Installing nest platforms in local wetlands can be an excellent community project, especially where heron populations are in decline.

NESTING: Great Blue Herons raise their young in rookeries consisting of several dozen mated pairs. The same group of trees with multiple large stick nests in each treetop is often reused year after year. Nests may eventually reach four feet in diameter. Male herons gather sticks from the ground and nearby trees, as well as from other nests. Females weave the nest and line it with softer materials, including pine needles, moss, reeds, and dry grass.

- **EGGS:** Three to six pale bluish-green to pale olive eggs; usually one brood.
- **EGG-LAYING:** Typically every two days.
- **INCUBATION:** Twenty-seven to twenty-nine days. Female starts incubating after the first egg is laid; in a clutch of five, the first chick hatched could be ten days older than the last.
- **DAYS TO FLEDGE:** First flight at seven to eight weeks. Parents may continue feeding chicks for another three weeks.

PLACEMENT: Great Blue Herons live in both freshwater and saltwater habitats, nesting in swamps or islands near forested marshes, rivers, lakes, seashores, and ponds. They are colonial nesters and like company. Place platforms at least thirty feet apart.

- **MOUNTING:** Artificial platforms of wood or metal can be mounted onto utility poles, tall four-by-four-inch wooden posts, or three lengths of ten-foot-long, two-and-one-quarter-inch-wide galvanized metal pipe coupled to create a thirty-foot pole. A set of three metal poles forms a sturdy tripod.
- **HEIGHT:** Place as high up as possible.

THE BUILD

GREAT BLUE HERON NESTING PLATFORM PLANS: The Lake County Audubon Society in Illinois has prepared a downloadable step-by-step booklet for building Great Blue Heron metal tripods and platforms. It's available at lakecountyaudubon.org.

The USGS Northern Prairie Wildlife Research Center offers woodworking plans for Great Blue Heron nesting platforms at npwrc.usgs.gov/resource/wildlife/ndblinds/gbheron.htm. (The plans are from the booklet *Building Nest Structures, Feeders and Photo Blinds* by Chris Grondahl and John Dockter.)

ROOKERY RESTORATION IN ILLINOIS

Dwindling Great Blue Heron populations at the Almond Marsh Forest Preserve in Grayslake, Illinois, concerned members of the local Lake County Audubon Society (LCAS). The bird's nesting trees had been rotting and falling down. To help restore the heron rookery, LCAS members decided, as a test, to build and install one human-made nesting platform. The Ascutney Mountain Audubon Society in Vermont provided them with metal tripod and nest basket plans. In February 2009, volunteers stood on the frozen marsh in the bitter cold and slowly raised an artificial "tree," a thirty-foot-tall metal pipe tripod topped with a basket platform and sunk deep into the marsh for stability. By spring, a Great Blue Heron pair had not only claimed the new site but also successfully fledged five chicks. In later years, eleven more nesting platforms were added, and in 2013, more platforms were fastened underneath several tripods. LCAS board member Jack Nowak notes that the platforms, "blend well into the marsh surroundings. You can hardly see them." But come spring, they are welcome sights to the fortunate herons that make the marsh their summer home.

Audubon volunteers trekked out onto the ice again in early 2013 to add more nesting platforms in hopes of attracting even more Great Blue Herons to the rookery.
Matt Enquist, courtesy of Conserve Lake County

Immature Great Blue Herons.
Ashok Khosla

A Great Blue Heron sits on its nest atop a dead tree in a northeast Texas lake.
Linda Cortelyou

Osprey

Pandion haliaetus

Sharp toes and talons help Ospreys hold on tight to fish, upon which they dine almost exclusively. *Ruhikanta Meetei*

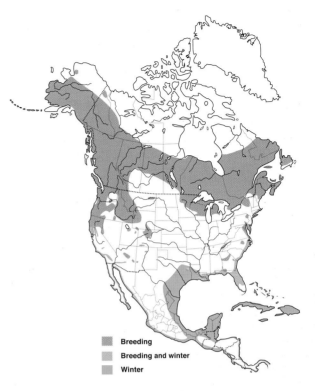

Breeding

Breeding and winter

Winter

Beginning in the early 1950s, Ospreys fell victim to pesticide poisoning that left their eggshells too thin to incubate. Populations plummeted. After the United States banned the pesticide DDT in 1972, coastal populations began to rebound. Today, chick deaths from entanglement in plastic fishing line and baling twine (used to bind bales of hay), which parent birds use as nesting materials, are increasingly common. Logging and shoreline development have made nesting sites scarce in some areas. Human-made nesting structures are crucial to many Osprey populations. Osprey reintroduction programs, which involve moving chicks from healthy populations to areas with depleted populations, have been successful.

RANGE: Ospreys are found on all continents except Antarctica. Most North American birds overwinter along the Gulf Coast and in Central and South America. The Chesapeake Bay, sometimes called "Osprey Garden," contains the highest density of breeding birds.

FIELD MARKS: These large, lanky "fish hawks" are brown above and white below, with slender bodies, long, narrow wings, and a white head with a broad brown stripe through the eye. Bent wings in flight appear M-shaped. Females are larger than males.

VOICE: The Osprey's high-pitched, whistling call is often given in a series—commonly *kyew-kyew-kyew*— that may rise in intensity as a threat increases. Ospreys are highly vocal.

FEEDING: The Osprey is the only North American raptor that preys almost exclusively on live fresh and saltwater fish. When searching for prey, Ospreys soar over water, hovering briefly before plunge-diving, feet first, to grab a fish. With long, sharp toes and talons, they position the slippery fish head forward to avoid wind resistance in flight. In Chesapeake Bay, menhaden is a key food; in Maine, mackerel and flounder make up most of the diet.

THE NEST SITE

HELP THROUGHOUT THE SEASONS: Ospreys readily—and in some areas exclusively—build nests on human structures, including telephone poles, channel markers, duck blinds, and specially designed open nesting platforms. Such structures play a vital role in restoring Osprey populations. People can also help prevent osprey chick deaths from entanglement by picking up and cutting up improperly discarded plastic twine and fishing line.

NESTING: Ospreys nest in exposed areas that provide an easy fly-in, including cliffs, tall snags, and treetops near open water. Unable to dive deeply, Ospreys prefer shallow fishing grounds. Males select the site and gather the many twigs, bark strips, grasses, and other detritus needed to construct the large stick nest. Females arrange

Cradle-shaped Osprey platforms are a common sight at the Blackwater National Wildlife Refuge on Maryland's Chesapeake Bay. Nesting platforms have helped sustain Osprey populations in this region, which supports the largest known concentration of Ospreys in the world; it is sometimes called the "Osprey Garden." *Mary Konchar*

An Osprey adds sticks to its nest. The platform and utility pole were donated and constructed by the Baltimore Gas and Electric Company as a way to keep Ospreys off the company's power lines. The new nest site is safer for the birds. *Michael S. Fitzpatrick, Baltimore Gas and Electric Company*

PROJECT OSPREY: BIRDS AND PEOPLE LIVING TOGETHER

In spring 2012, the city of Stoughton, Wisconsin, had to act quickly. Ospreys were nesting atop a light pole in Mandt Park and had woven sticks in between the megawatt sports lights. These sticks could act like kindling once the lights were turned on for baseball games. The mayor's office, city parks, fire department, utility company, and residents came up with a plan to save the Ospreys from their hazardous home. While the Ospreys were away from the nest, a donat-ed four-by-four-foot wooden platform was placed five feet away from the lights and filled with the Osprey's own nesting sticks. Madison Audubon member and Wild Birds Unlimited employee Pat Ready consulted on the project and said it was a team effort. "The city of Stoughton and its individuals were responsive to Osprey needs," Ready says. "We all came together for the birds." The reward? The Osprey pair fledged two chicks.

This Osprey pair was determined to build a nest on top of a megawatt light post in a busy Wisconsin city park. *Patrick Ready*

To help out the Ospreys and prevent a potential fire, the Stoughton, Wisconsin, fire department installed a new nesting platform for the Ospreys, a safe distance away from the hot lights. *Patrick Ready*

The new nesting platform suits the Ospreys just fine. In spite of the noisy baseball games and carnivals below, the Ospreys managed to fledge two chicks. *Patrick Ready*

the nesting material. Reused nests may eventually reach six feet in diameter.

- **EGGS:** One to four, usually three, beige to cinnamon, reddish-brown spotted, hen-sized eggs. One brood per season.
- **EGG-LAYING:** One or two days apart.
- **INCUBATION:** Thirty-six to forty-two days. Birds hatch in the order laid.
- **DAYS TO FLEDGE:** Fifty to fifty-five days. If food is abundant, all chicks may survive; if not, younger chicks may starve.

PLACEMENT: Ospreys prefer nesting in the tallest trees, near water with abundant fish supplies. They are found near shallow coastal waters. Inland, they nest in and around lakes, rivers, and reservoirs.

- **MOUNTING:** Attach platforms to wooden utility poles or metal tripods.
- **HEIGHT:** Ospreys have successfully nested on cell phone towers as high as 150 feet. Place nesting platforms as high as possible.

THE BUILD

OSPREY ARTIFICIAL NESTING PLATFORM PLANS: Many state natural resources departments provide Osprey nesting platform plans.

A simple Osprey platform construction drawing is available on the Wisconsin Department of Natural Resources website, dnr.wi.gov/files/pdf/pubs/er/er0680.pdf.

CHAPTER 5

HOW TO HELP THE BIRDS

Today, those interested in helping nesting birds have more company than ever. Using the power of the Internet, scientists are making use of willing volunteers, called "citizen scientists," to collaborate across the continents in making ornithological observations. Citizen scientists record their data and submit it online, often achieving a breadth of observations that could never be attained by research teams alone. Many bird organizations are using citizen science to supplement their research efforts. Having a multitude of data on hand puts scientists and policy makers in a better position to advocate for legislative changes that will help birds.

REALITY TV FOR THE BIRDS

One recent tool now enhancing many birders' enjoyment of their favorite subjects is the "bird cam," a specialized video camera fitted inside a nest box or near an active nesting platform. Bird cams allow first-hand viewing of nesting birds over the Internet or closed circuit monitors—a kind of avian reality TV. They are a great way to get up close and personal with bird families and to learn more about nesting bird behavior as well as the challenges nesting birds face each breeding season. Many bird organizations, including the Cornell Lab of Ornithology and National Audubon Society, host bird cams.

Seen in this screen shot, a heron adult, its beak low to the nest, awaits the hatching of its chicks. Hundreds of thousands of people from more than 160 countries have tuned in to the Cornell Lab of Ornithology's "Heron Cam" since it debuted in spring 2012. Viewers have witnessed little-known events such as heron courtship and watched live as five tiny Great Blue Herons, over the course of several days, pipped themselves out of their shells. A Great Horned Owl attack early one morning recorded rarely heard heron defensive screams that seemed to keep the owl at bay. The Lab's Bird Cams program includes other species, too. To watch the shows, visit allaboutbirds.org/cams. *Courtesy of the Cornell Lab of Ornithology*

In collaboration with Explore.org, this "Osprey Cam" (upper left) was added to the artificial nesting platform during the summer of 2012 at the Hog Island Audubon Camp in Maine (hogisland.audubon.org). Though campers viewed the nest platform itself from a respectable distance on camp property, they also gathered regularly around the Osprey Cam's TV monitor in the dining hall. That way they got up-close views of the Osprey chicks as they progressed from eggs to fledglings. Thousands of people across the globe kept up with the chicks at their own computers. *Stephen W. Kress*

Although bird cam websites continually change over time as cameras are added or taken down, the home pages on the websites of hosting organizations are good places to find links to up-and-running bird cam sites. YouTube videos taken from bird cams also provide a twenty-first century peek into the lives of nesting birds.

BIRD CONSERVATION ORGANIZATIONS

AMERICAN BIRD CONSERVANCY:
ABCBIRDS.ORG, 540-253-5780

The American Bird Conservancy's focus is the protection of native bird species and their habitats throughout the Americas. The group's "Cats Indoors" program—designed to help reduce bird mortality caused by outdoor cats—was developed as part of a larger effort to reduce threats to birds.

BIRD STUDIES CANADA:
BIRDSCANADA.ORG, 888-448-2473

Canada's national charitable organization for bird science and conservation, Bird Studies Canada, advances the understanding, appreciation, and conservation of wild birds and their habitats. Each year, more than 30,000 volunteers participate in this organization's citizen science initiatives. Programs include Project FeederWatch, the Christmas Bird Count, the Great Backyard Bird Count, the Canadian Lakes Loon Survey, regionally based breeding bird atlases, nocturnal owl surveys, and marsh-monitoring programs.

CORNELL LAB OF ORNITHOLOGY:
BIRDS.CORNELL.EDU, 800-843-2473

Founded in 1915, the Cornell Lab of Ornithology's mission is to interpret and conserve the Earth's biological diversity through research, education, and citizen science focused on birds. Lab-sponsored citizen science programs, including eBird, YardMap, Project FeederWatch, NestWatch, Celebrate Urban Birds, and the annual Great Backyard Bird Count, engage the general public in hands-on learning experiences, while collecting valuable data for ornithological research. The Lab also hosts Birds of North America Online, bna.birds.cornell.edu/bna, available by subscription. This comprehensive, continuously updated collection of researcher-written species accounts includes more than 700 birds that breed in the United States and Canada.

HAWK MOUNTAIN SANCTUARY:
HAWKMOUNTAIN.ORG, 610-756-6961

The Hawk Mountain Sanctuary in Kempton, Pennsylvania, is a scientific research center focusing on raptor conservation and education. It is also one of the best places in the eastern United States to watch the fall hawk migration. Early work using nest boxes to study American Kestrels started at Hawk Mountain and continues today. Sanctuary founder Rosalie Edge's vision is reflected in a quote often cited by the sanctuary: "The time to protect a species is while it is still common."

NATIONAL AUDUBON SOCIETY:
AUDUBON.ORG, 800-876-0994

Named for John James Audubon, who painted and described numerous North American birds nearly two centuries ago, the National Audubon Society was incorporated in 1905. Today, Audubon is made up of more than 500,000 members and nearly 500 local chapters, where people interested in birds can work together for their benefit. State offices, sanctuaries, education centers, and summer camps are all part of the organization's education and conservation mission. The real-time, online bird checklist program, eBird, is co-sponsored by Audubon and the Cornell Lab of Ornithology. The Audubon Christmas Bird Count, begun on December 25, 1900, is perhaps North America's oldest citizen science effort, producing continuous, vital information on bird populations.

ORGANIZATIONS FOR SPECIFIC BIRDS MENTIONED IN THIS BOOK

Bluebirds

NORTH AMERICAN BLUEBIRD SOCIETY:
NABLUEBIRDSOCIETY.ORG

Since 1978, the North American Bluebird Society (NABS) has promoted the prosperity and recovery of bluebirds and other cavity-nesting birds throughout North America. The group awards education, conservation, and research grants that further this mission. NABS offers online guidelines for safely maintaining nest boxes and fostering healthy birds, an online catalog of books and educational materials for sale, and the quarterly journal *Bluebird*. Their annual conference is co-hosted each year by one of its fifty-eight affiliate groups, which include many state and provincial bluebird organizations.

Purple Martin

PURPLE MARTIN CONSERVATION ASSOCIATION:
PURPLEMARTIN.ORG, 814-833-7656

Founded in 1987, the Purple Martin Conservation Association (PMCA) is dedicated to the conservation and scientific study of Purple Martins. Specific research projects look at martin colony locations, biology, and habitat

A young kestrel protests the banding process; however, leg bands are a valuable research tool. The bird will soon be released to soar over this Pennsylvania farmland. *Courtesy of Hawk Mountain Sanctuary*

A male and female Eastern Bluebird start to build a nest in the XBox. *David Kinneer*

requirements. The "Purple Martin Mentor" program connects martin "newbies" with veteran Purple Martin "landlords," and an online forum keeps landlords in touch with each other. The online "Martin Market Place" sells recommended martin housing and accouterments.

Wood Duck
WOOD DUCK SOCIETY:
WOODDUCKSOCIETY.COM

The Minnesota-based Wood Duck Society works to educate and promote sound management for Wood Duck populations. Detailed methods for safe and successful Wood Duck nest box installation and placement are included in the online document *Best Practices*. The society's newsletter, *The Wood Duck Newsgram*, is published three times a year.

Burrowing Owl
BURROWING OWL CONSERVATION NETWORK:
BURROWINGOWLCONSERVATION.ORG

This nonprofit's mission is to promote Burrowing Owl conservation and showcase successful, innovative solutions that can be applied throughout Burrowing Owl habitat in North America. Working with the city of Antioch, California, the group established the twenty-four-acre Prewett Family Park Burrowing Owl Preserve in 2008. At the time, no owls occupied the site. In 2012, five owl pairs successfully fledged twenty-six chicks. Today, the preserve includes both natural and artificial burrows, a weed-management program, interpretive signs, and an education and field trip program for local students.

Chimney Swift
THE DRIFTWOOD WILDLIFE ASSOCIATION:
CHIMNEYSWIFTS.ORG

The Driftwood Wildlife Association (DWA), located in Austin, Texas, promotes public education about Chimney Swifts, preservation of their existing habitat, and the creation of new nesting and roosting sites. Directors Georgean and Paul Kyle founded Travis Audubon's Chaetura Canyon Bird Sanctuary, where Chimney Swift research has taken place since the 1980s. DWA's website contains news about Chimney Swift research projects, links to Chimney Swift tower construction videos, and listings for events such as A Swift Night Out.

Common Loon
THE LOON PRESERVATION COMMITTEE:
LOON.ORG

One of the first U.S. groups to work for loon conservation, the Loon Preservation Committee was founded in 1975 in response to dramatically declining loon populations. The group's research focuses on how human activities impact loons, with the goal of restoring New Hampshire's loon populations.

CITIZEN SCIENCE PROJECTS INVOLVING NESTING BIRDS
AMERICAN KESTREL PARTNERSHIP:
PEREGRINEFUND.ORG, 208-362-3716

The American Kestrel Partnership, a project begun in 2011 by the Peregrine Fund, promotes the use of kestrel nest boxes by people all over the country. These nest boxes not only enhance kestrel habitat but also create valuable

These Barred Owlets, just more than a month old, are on an out-of-nest box adventure. Each bird will be banded as part of a research project. They will return to the nest box for another week or so, until the urge to leave becomes strong. *Rob Bierregaard*

An artificial Chimney Swift tower. *Kelly Applegate*

study sites. The group seeks to discover the causes of regional kestrel declines; they believe data from kestrel nest box observers may help reveal answers. The project's interactive website offers training and social networking opportunities with like-minded kestrel watchers.

CORNELL LAB OF ORNITHOLOGY'S NESTWATCH: NESTWATCH.ORG

NestWatch is the place to go to learn more about nesting birds, as well as monitor bird nests for science. Participants in this nationwide program, called NestWatchers, collect information on when nesting occurs, numbers of eggs laid, egg hatch rates, and chick survival rates. Participation is free and online instructions are provided. Studies based on NestWatch data are yielding clues about breeding bird populations and how they are changing over time due to factors including climate change and habitat degradation.

NORTH AMERICAN BREEDING BIRD SURVEY: PWRC.USGS.GOV/BBS

This survey, a collaboration begun in 1966 between the U.S. Geological Survey's Patuxent Wildlife Research Center and the Canadian Wildlife Service, monitors the status of North American bird populations. At the peak of every breeding season, more than 2,500 skilled birders, who are able to identify local birds by sound, collect data along thousands of randomly established roadside routes throughout the continent. Survey coordinators, researchers, and statisticians then compile and deliver population data and population trend analyses on more than 400 bird species, for use by conservation managers, scientists, and the general public.

PURPLE MARTIN CONSERVATION ASSOCIATION'S PROJECT MARTINWATCH AND SCOUT-ARRIVAL STUDY: PURPLEMARTIN.ORG/MAIN/RESEARCH.HTML

Project MartinWatch is a continentwide venture in which active Purple Martin "landlords" are provided with nest record forms to fill out as they conduct weekly nest checks on the martins breeding in their houses or gourds. Another project, the Scout-arrival Study, tracks the northward migration of Purple Martins across the continent each spring. Landlords send in the date that "scouts"—the oldest martins that are first to return to their breeding grounds—are first seen.

TO LEARN MORE ABOUT BUILDING NEST BOXES: NESTBOXBUILDER.COM

Georgia woodworker Fred Stille puts "bird-approved" nest box construction plans and woodworking tips all in one place on this site—just what he was looking for when he first got into building for birds.

TO LEARN MORE ABOUT CAVITY-NESTING BIRDS: SIALIS.ORG

Connecticut bluebirder Bet Zimmerman's popular website includes information about cavity-nesting birds, nest and egg identification, and bird-oriented online forums and listservs, as well as good advice for "bluebird emergencies."

TO LEARN NESTING BIRD SONGS: BIRDJAM.COM

BIBLIOGRAPHY

Baicich, Paul J., Colin J. O. Harrison. *A Guide to the Nests, Eggs, and Nestlings of North American Birds.* 2nd ed. Princeton, NJ: Princeton University Press, 2005.

Baynes, Ernest Harold. *Wild Bird Guests: How to Entertain Them.* New York: E. P. Dutton and Co., 1915.

Berger, Cynthia, Keith Kridler, and Jack Griggs. *The Bluebird Monitor's Guide.* New York: Harper Collins, 2001.

Dearborn, Ned. *Bird Houses and How to Build Them.* Farmer's Bulletin 609: U.S. Department of Agriculture, 1914.

Forbush, Edward Howe. *Useful Birds and Their Protection.* Massachusetts State Board of Agriculture, 1907.

Henderson, Carrol L. *Woodworking for Wildlife: Homes for Birds and Animals.* 3rd ed. St. Paul, MN: State of Minnesota Department of Administration, Materials Management Division, 2009 (third edition).

Kalmbach, E. R., W. L. McAtee. *Homes for Birds.* Farmer's Bulletin 1456: U.S. Department of Agriculture, 1930.

Kress, Stephen W. *The Audubon Society Guide to Attracting Birds.* New York: Charles Scribner's Sons, 1985.

——— *The Audubon Society Guide to Attracting Birds: Creating Natural Habitats for Properties Large and Small.* Ithaca, NY: Cornell University Press, 2006.

Schutz, Walter E. *Bird Watching, Housing and Feeding.* Milwaukee, WI: The Bruce Publishing Company, 1963.

Sorlie, Kip, and Richard Schinkel. *Building for Birds.* Berrien Springs, MI: White-throat Images, 1988.

Stokes, Donald W., Lillian Q. Stokes. *The Complete Birdhouse Book.* Boston: Little, Brown and Company, 1990.

Terres, John K. *Songbirds in Your Garden.* Chapel Hill, NC: Algonquin Books of Chapel Hill, 1994.

Trafton, Gilbert H. *Methods of Attracting Birds.* Boston: Houghton Mifflin, 1910.

ONLINE SOURCES

"All About Birds," Hugh Powell, editor, 2013, Ithaca, NY: Cornell Laboratory of Ornithology, allaboutbirds.org.

"The Birds of North America Online." A. Poole, editor, Ithaca, NY: Cornell Laboratory of Ornithology, 2005, bna.birds.cornell.edu/bna/

"Homes for Birds," Department of the Interior: U.S. Fish and Wildlife Service: Conservation Library, 2010, library.fws.gov/bird_publications/house.html

National Geographic: Backyard Birding, Animals.nationalgeographic.com/animals/birding

North American Bluebird Society, 2013, nabluebirdsociety.org.

Purple Martin Conservation Association, 2013, purplemartin.org.

Stille, Fred, NestboxBuilder.com, 2013, nestboxbuilder.com.

Zimmerman, Elizabeth A., Sialis.org, 2013, sialis.org.

INDEX

Page numbers in italics after a bird species indicate the profile pages for that species. Page numbers in italics after a nest box name indicate the plans for that nest box.

Abare, Chuck, 26, 115, 117–119
Aix sponsa (Wood Duck), 16, 21, 30, *106–107*
Althea R. Sherman Project, 15
American Bird Conservancy, 153
American Kestrel, *91–93*, 154–155
American Kestrel nest box, 21, 27, *94–95*, 96–98
American Kestrel Partnership, 154–155
American Ornithologist's Union, 10
American Robin, 120, 121, *129–130*
ants, 29
Ardea herodias (Great Blue Heron), 120, 121, *146–147*
Ascutney Mountain Audubon Society (Vermont), 148
Ash-throated Flycatcher, *57–58*
Athene cunicularia (Burrowing Owl), 120, *138–139*
Audubon, John James, 153
Audubon Minnesota, 144

Baeolophus atricristatus (Black-crested Titmouse), *63*
Baeolophus bicolor (Tufted Titmouse), *61*
Baeolophus inornatus (Oak Titmouse), *62*
Baeolophus ridgwayi (Juniper Titmouse), *62*
baffles. *See* predator guards
Bald Eagle, 120
Barn Owl, 11, *84–85*
Barn Owl nest box, 29, *86–87*
Barn Swallow, 120, *126–127*
Barred Owl, *64–65*
Barred Owl box, *66–67*, 68–70
Baynes, Ernest Harold, 10
bees, 29
Bellrose, Frank, 16
Belthoff, James R., 140
Berner, Kevin, 51
Bewick's Wren, *34*
Bierregaard, Richard O., 65–70
bird cams, 152–153
birdhouse basics. *See* homebuilding basics
birdhouse flaws, 18–19
birdjam.com, 155
Bird Studies Canada, 153
Black-capped Chickadee, *99–101*
Black-crested Titmouse, *63*
black flies, 28
blowflies, 28
Bluebird Recovery Program (BBRP) of Minnesota, 50
bluebirds, 14, 16, 30, 32, 46–56, 121, 153
    bluebird Xbox, 22, *52–53*, 54–56, 58, 60, 63
    Eastern Bluebird, 16, 46, *47–49*

Mountain Bluebird, 46, *49*
    nest site/placement, 50–51
    Western Bluebird, 46, *48–49*
Bower, Allen, 80–83
Bower Flicker box, *80–81*, 82–83
Bronson, Cindy, 101
buffalo gnats, 28
Burrowing Owl, 120, *138–139*, 154
Burrowing Owl Conservation Network, 140, 154

Canadian Wildlife Service, 155
Carolina Chickadee, *99–101*
Carolina Wren, *34–35*
Carolina Wren nest box, 36, *37*, 38–39
Carpodacus mexicanus (House Finch), 120, *134–135*
cats, 12–13, 23
    outdoor enclosures for, 23–24
    predator guards for, 23
    as predators, 12–13
caulks, 21
Center for Conservation Biology (Williamsburg, VA), 10
Chaetura pelagica (Chimney Swift), 10, 15, 16, 120, *143–145*
Chickadee nest box, *102–103*, 104–105
chickadees, 16, 30, 32, 46, 99–105
    Black-capped Chickadee, *99–101*
    Carolina Chickadee, *99–101*
    Chickadee nest box, *102–103*, 104–105
    Mountain Chickadee, *100–101*
    nest site/placement, 100–101
Chimney Swift, 10, 15, 16, 120, *143–145*
    Chimney Swift towers, 145
    The Driftwood Wildlife Association (DWA), 154
    nest site/location, 143–145
Chuck's Simple Purple Martin Rack, *117*, 118–119
closure nails, 21
Colaptes auratus (Northern Flicker), *78–79*
Comfort, Tom, 51
Common Loon, 120, *141–142*, 154
Connecticut Audubon Society, 13
construction
    of floors, 19
    types of poor, 19
construction flaws, 19
Cornell Lab of Ornithology, 29, 31, 101, 152, 153, 155
Covered shelf for American Robins, *132*, 133
cowbirds, 41

Dearborn, Ned, 12, 14

Delaware County Bird Club, 93
Dockter, John, 147
Don "The Duckman's" Wood Duck Nest Box, *108–109*, 110–111, 113
door pivots, 21
doves, 122–125
    Mourning Dove nest basket, *124*, 125
    nest site/placement, 122–123
drainage holes, 22
The Driftwood Wildlife Association (DWA), 154
ducks, 106–111
    Don "The Duckman's" Wood Duck Nest Box, *108–109*, 110–111
    nest site/placement, 107
    Wood Duck, 16, 21, 30, *106–107*, 154

Eastern Bluebird, 16, 46, *47*
Eastern Phoebe, *136–137*
Eastern Screech-Owl, *71–73*
Eastern Screech-Owl nest box, *74–75*, 76–77
English Sparrow. *See* House Sparrow
Eno, Steve, 51
Environmental Protection Agency (EPA), 12
European Starling
    active controls for, 27
    passive controls for, 26
    as predators, 12, 14, 16, 25–26, 46
    SREHs, 26
Explore.org, 152

Falco sparverius (American Kestrel), *91–93*
feeders, 14
finches, 121, 134–135
    House Finch, 120, *134–135*
    nest site/placement, 135
finishes
    for homebuilding, 21
    not recommended, 18–19
fire ants, 29
fleas, 29
flicker, 78–83
    Bower Flicker box, *80–81*, 82–83
    nest site/location, 79
    Northern Flicker, *78–79*
flycatcher, 16, 57–58
    Ash-throated Flycatcher, *57–58*
    Great Crested Flycatcher, *57–58*
    nest site/placement, 58
Forbush, Edward Howe, 13
Friends of the Sherman Swift Tower, 15

Gallo, Susan, 142
Gavia immer (Common Loon), 120, *141–142*

Gehlbach, Frederick R., 20, 72, 74–77
Gilbertson, Steve, 22, 51
Gilbertson pole system, 22, 23, 51, 58, 60
Gilbertson PVC nest box, 22
Gillis, Donald C., 140
Gilwood nest box, 22
glues, 21
gnatcatchers, 121
Goldfinches, 19
Great Blue Heron, 120, 121, *146–147*
Great Crested Flycatcher, *57–58*
Great Horned Owl, 89, 152
Gregg, Michael A., 140
Grondahl, Chris, 147
Grubb, Tom, 101
Grubb stakes, 101

Hawkins, Art, 16
Hawk Mountain Sanctuary, 153
Helmeke, Don, 108–111
Henderson, Carrol L., 140
Her, Johnny, 144
herons, 146–148
    Great Blue Heron, 120, 121, *146–147*
    nesting platforms, 147
    nest site/placement, 147
Higgins, Phil, 140
hinges, 21
homebuilding basics
    access, 22
    caulks and glues, 21
    drainage holes, 22
    fasteners, 20
    finishes, 21
    hinges, pivots, and closure nails, 21
    overhanging roofs, 22
    placement of nest boxes, 22–23
    tools, 20
    ventilation, 21–22
    woods for, 19–20
Hooded Merganser, 16, *112–113*
hornets, 29
House Finch, 120, *134–135*
housekeeping, 31, 45
House Sparrow
    active controls, 27
    passive controls for, 26
    as predators, 12, 13–14, 16, 25–26, 46
House Wren, 27–28, *34–35*
humans
    as helpers for birds, 14–17, 121
    as threats to birds, 11–12
hummingbirds, 121
Hungry Owl Project (HOP), 11
hurricanes, 10
Hutchings, Don, 24
Hutchings' predator guard, 23–24

insect pests, 28–29, 31

Johnson, David H., 140
juncos, 121

Juniper Titmouse, *62*

Kalmbach, E. R., 14
kestrel, 91–98
    American Kestrel, *91–93*, 154–155
    American Kestrel nest box, 21, 27, *94–95*,
        96–98
    nest site/placement, 92–93
Kress, Steve, 128, 130–133
Kridler, Keith, 51
Kyle, Georgean Z., 145
Kyle, Paul D., 145

Lake County Audubon Society (Illinois),
    147–148
lice, 29
Lincer, Jeffrey L., 140
Linn, Sherry, 31
The Loon Network, 142
The Loon Preservation Committee, 154
loons, 141–142
    Common Loon, 120, *141–142*, 154
    nest site/placement, 141–142
Lophodytes cucullatus (Hooded Merganser),
    112–113
Los Angeles Audubon Society, 121
L-shaped platform for Barn Swallows, *128*

Madison Audubon, 150
Maine Loon Project (Audubon), 142
McAtee, W. L., 14
McEwen, Charles, 26
Mennill, Daniel, 101
mergansers, 112–113
    Hooded Merganser, *112–113*
    nest site/placement, 112–113
Michigan Bluebird Society, 23
Migratory Bird Treaty Act, 12, 27
Minnesota Bluebird Recovery Group, 22
Minnesota Purple Martin Working
    Group, 116
Minnesota Waterfowl Association, 111
mites, 29
Mountain Bluebird, 46, *49*
Mountain Chickadee, *100–101*
Mourning Dove, 120, *122–123*
Mourning Dove nest basket, *124*, 125
Musselman, Thomas Edgar, 14, 16
Myiarchus cinerascens (Ash-throated
    Flycatcher), *57–58*
Myiarchus crinitus (Great Crested Flycatcher),
    57–58

National Audubon Society, 152, 153
natural threats to birds, 10–11
nest box basics. *See* homebuilding basics
nestboxbuilder.com, 155
nest checks, 29–31
NestWatch (Cornell Lab of Ornithology),
    155
Noel hardware cloth guard, 25
North American Bluebird Association, 31

North American Bluebird Society (NABS),
    16, 51, 82, 153
North American Breeding Bird Survey, 155
Northern Flicker, *78–79*
Northern Prairie Wildlife Research Center
    (USGS), 124–125, 147
Nowak, Jack, 148
nuthatches, 32

Oak Titmouse, *62*
Ohio Bluebird Society, 36
orioles, 121
Orthwein, Bob, 36–39
Osprey, 120, *149–151*
    artificial platforms, 151
    nest site/placement, 149, 151
    Project Osprey (Stoughton, WI), 150–151
Otter, Ken, 101
Otus asio (Eastern Screech-Owl), *71–73*
Otus kennicottii (Western Screech-Owl),
    71–73
owls, 30, 64–77, 84–90, 138–140
    Barn Owl, *84–85*
    Barred Owl, *64–65*
    Barred Owl box, *66–67*, 68–70
    Burrowing Owl, 120, *138–139*, 154
    Eastern Screech-Owl, *71–73*
    Great Horned Owl, 89, 152
    nest site/placement, 65, 73, 84–85, 139
    Screech-Owl nest box, *74–75*, 76–77
    Western Screech-Owl, *71–73*

painting, 18–19
Pandion haliaetus (Osprey), 120, *149–151*
paper wasps, 28
parasites, 29, 31
Passer domesticus (House Sparrow), 12,
    13–14, 16, 25–26
Patuxent Wildlife Research Center
    (U.S.Geological Survey), 155
perches, 19
pesticides, 11, 12
Peterson, Dick, 22, 29, 50
Phillips, Dick, 93
phoebes, 120, 130–133, 136–137
    Eastern Phoebe, *136–137*
    nest site/placement, 137
    Say's Phoebe, *136–137*
Pike, Nicholas, 13
Poecile atricapilla (Black-capped Chickadee),
    99–101
Poecile carolinensis (Carolina Chickadee),
    99–101
Poecile gambeli (Mountain Chickadee),
    100–101
predator guards, 13, 23
predators
    cats, 12–13, 23
    checking for, 29–30
    European Starlings, 12, 14
    House Sparrows, 12, 13–14
    House Wrens, 27–28
    raccoons, 22, 24–25

snakes, 12, 22, 25
squirrels, 26
Progne subis (Purple Martin), 16, 21, 26, *114–116*
Project MartinWatch, 155
Prothonotary Warbler, *40*
Prothonotary warbler nest box, 42–45
Protonotaria citrea (Prothonotary Warbler), *40*
pruning, 121
Purple Martin, 16, 21, 26, *114–116*, 153–154
    nest site/placement, 115–116
    Purple Martin Wooden Gourd Rack, *117*, 118–119
Purple Martin Conservation Association, 115, 153–154, 155
Purple Martin Wooden Gourd Rack, *117*, 118–119

raccoons, 22, 24–26
Radel, Keith, 22, 50, 51
Raptor On! Kestrel nest box, 21, 27, *94–95*, 96–98
Ready, Pat, 150
Rebholz, James L., 140
recycled materials, nest boxes from, 19
Red-cockaded Woodpecker, 10
Reilly, Bob, 41–45
Richmond Audubon Society, 41
robins, 129–133
    American Robin, 120, 121, *129–130*
    Covered shelf for American Robins, *132*, 133
    nest site/placement, 129–130
    V-shaped shelf for American Robins, *130*, 131

Santa Clara Valley Audubon Society, 140
Sayornis phoebe (Eastern Phoebe), *136–137*
Sayornis saya (Say's Phoebe), *136–137*
Say's Phoebe, *136–137*
Schieffelin, Eugene, 14
Schinkel, Dick, 17
Scout-arrival Study (Purple Martin Conservation Association), 155
Screech-Owl, 20
Screech-Owl nest box, *74–75*, 76–77
Seekamp, Ron, 116
Sherman, Althea Rosina, 15
Sialia currucoides (Mountain Bluebird), 46, *49*
Sialia mexicana (Western Bluebird), 46, *48*
Sialia sialis (Eastern Bluebird), 16, 46, *47*
sialis.org, 155
Simmons, Steve, 29, 31, 86–90, 89, 140
Simple Wooden Gourd Rack, 115
Smithsonian Conservation Biology Institute, 12
snakes
    predator guards for, 25
    as predators, 12, 22
    traps for, 25
snow, 10–11

Sparks, Dan, 51–56
sparrows, 121
squirrels, 26
SREHs, 26
Stille, Fred, 51, 155
Stovall, Bill, 17
Strand, Roger, 21
Strix varia (Barred Owl), *64–65*
Sturnus vulgaris (European Starling), 12, 14, 16, 25–26
swallows, 16, 46, 59–60, 121, 126–128
    Barn Swallow, 120, *126–127*
    L-shaped platform for Barn Swallows, *128*
    nest site/placement, 60, 126–127
    Tree Swallow, 30, 41, 46, *59–60*
    Violet-green Swallow, *59–60*

Tachycineta bicolor (Tree Swallow), 30, 41, 46, *59–60*
Tachycineta thalassina (Violet-green Swallow), *59–60*
Temple, Stan, 12
Texas Bluebird Society, 21
threats to birds
    human, 11–12
    from introduced species, 12–14
    natural, 10–11
thrushes, 121
Thryomanes bewickii (Bewick's Wren), *34*
Thryothorus ludovicianus (Carolina Wren), 34, *35*
ticks, 29
titmice, 16, 30, 46, 61–66
    Black-crested Titmouse, *63*
    Juniper Titmouse, *62*
    nest site/placement, 62–63
    Oak Titmouse, *62*
    Tufted Titmouse, *61*
tools
    for homebuilding, 20
    for nest box maintenance, 31
    for nest checks, 30
tree pruning, 121
Tree Swallows, 30, 41, 46, *59–60*
Troglodytes aedon (House Wren), 27–28, *34–35*
Tufted Titmouse, *61*
Turdus migratorius (American Robin), 120, 121, *129–130*
Tuttle, Dick, 21, 27, 93–98
Tyto alba (Barn Owl), *84–85*

U.S. Bureau of Biological Survey, 14
U.S. Department of Agriculture, 12
U.S. Fish and Wildlife Institute, 12
U.S. Fish and Wildlife Service, 12, 16
U.S. Geological Survey, 155

Vaux's Swift, 143
ventilation, 21–22
Vermont Loon Recovery Project, 142
Violet-green Swallow, *59–60*
vireos, 121

V-shaped nest for American Robins, *130*, 131

warblers, 19, 40–45, 121
    location/placement, 40–41
    Prothonotary Warbler, *40*
    Prothonotary warbler nest box, *42–43*, 44–45
Watts, Bryan, 10
Western Bluebird, 46, *48*
Western Screech-Owl, *71–73*
WildCare, 11
Willett, Chris, 16, 20–22, 101–105, 128, 130–133
Windingstad, Ron, 144
Wisconsin Department of Natural Resources, 151
Wood Duck, 16, 21, 30, *106–107*, 154
Wood Duck nest box, *108–109*, 110–111, 113
Wood Duck Society, 21, 111, 154
woodpeckers, 32, 121
woods, 19–20
woodworking
    Stovall birdhouses, 17
wrens, 16, 34–39, 121
    Bewick's Wren, *34*
    Carolina Wren, *34–35*
    Carolina Wren nest box, *37*, 38–39
    House Wren, 27–28, *34–35*
    nest site/placement, 36

Xbox, 22, *52–53*, 54–56, 58, 60, 63

yellow jackets, 29

Zeleny, Lawrence, 16
Zeleny, Olive, 16
Zenaida macroura (Mourning Dove), 120, *122–123*
Zimmerman, Bet, 30, 155

ABOUT THE TEAM

Woodworker Chris Willett attaches a predator guard baffle to a nest box pole.

Authors Elissa Wolfson (l) and Margaret A. Barker carry Chuck's Simple Wooden Gourd Rack for purple martins.

MARGARET A. BARKER is a writer and educator in the Chesapeake Bay region. Following a broadcast journalism career in the Southeast, she received a master's degree in environmental education. She served as coordinator of the Cornell Laboratory of Ornithology's Project FeederWatch and later managed the Kids Growing Food school garden program for Cornell University Department of Education. She wrote the "Backyard Birding" column for the *Ithaca Journal* newspaper for seven years and co-authored (with Jack Griggs) *The FeederWatcher's Guide to Bird Feeding* (HarperCollins, 2000). Her work has appeared in publications such as *Birdwatching* (formerly *Birder's World)* and *Bird Watcher's Digest*.

ELISSA WOLFSON is a freelance writer and editor for a variety of science, environmental, botanical, ornithological, and animal-related publications. After receiving a bachelor's degree from Cornell University, she worked as an environmental educator for nearly a decade prior to receiving a master's from Montclair State College and transitioning into environmental journalism. Editorial clients have included the National Audubon Society, Cornell University Laboratory of Ornithology, and Cornell University College of Veterinary Medicine. She is the author of the book *101 Cool Games for Cool Cats* (Rockwell House, 2007)and a former editor of *E: The Environmental Magazine* and *Cornell Plantations Magazine*.

STEPHEN KRESS, author of *The Audubon Society Guide to Attracting Birds*, is vice president for bird conservation for the National Audubon Society and director of the Hog Island Audubon Camp. He also teaches a popular birding course at the Cornell Laboratory of Ornithology. As director of Audubon's Project Puffin, he has restored puffins and other rare and endangered seabirds to islands on the Maine coast and other locations worldwide. Taking his interest in bird restoration to backyards and larger habitats, he has developed methods for creating bird-friendly habitats using nest boxes and native plants.

CHRIS WILLETT is a craftsman and contractor in upstate New York, specializing in green building techniques, energy efficiency, and solar technologies. His academic work in environmental studies at Ithaca College has included researching the effects of avian malaria on native Hawaiian bird populations, working to protect and preserve the endangered Marianas Crow's habitat in the Northern Marianas Islands, and banding raptors throughout New York state. He is currently developing a new business, Bird Brain Bungalows (www.bird-brain-bungalows.com), in order to create ecologically sound and efficient homes for many avian species, as well as flying mammals and honeybees.